ELIOT COUVAT

The Social Token Revolution

The next big thing in crypto is here, and it will revolutionize how people work together.

This book was professionally typeset on Reedsy.
Find out more at reedsy.com

Contents

Preface

Innovation in Crypto has led us to a new era that will revolutionize how we make money and collaborate. Indeed, DAOs, NFT, Web3 & Social Tokens will allow talented individuals to collaborate and work on smaller-scale projects in a trustful way. Those new technologies allow creating trust between collaborators worldwide without having to create legal entities. It unleashes a new world of possibilities by facilitating coordination at scale. A whole ecosystem of tools is being built around these technologies, and millions of individuals will soon earn a living by exploring their curiosity and contributing to different projects simultaneously.

We're leaning toward a more fluid way of working. Individuals will follow their interests, collaborating on multiple projects simultaneously, without having the constraint of working at a company (hierarchy, office hours, silo...). We're seeing this unbundling of traditional employment happening in front of our eyes. As a society, we have to re-invent the way we work, interact socially, communicate, and ensure comfort and security at work.

Social Token is a complete paradigm shift in the way people will work and collaborate. This book aims to give an overview of the fundamental concepts around Social Tokens and educate the next millions of workers to leverage crypto mechanisms, understand the technical aspects of Web3 and explore the potential future we will live in.

Since I'm working full-time in Web3, my goal has always been to educate and onboard new people in the social token space. Innovation in Crypto (DAOs, NFT, Defi, Web3 & Social Tokens) has led us to a new era that will revolutionize almost every area of our lives, from how we make money to how we collaborate.

Education plays a significant role in the mass adoption of all those new concepts, and this book aims to participate in making this one-in-a-generation change happens.

As more people are leaping Web3, I received many questions and requests on how to understand this space better. I've written this book to answer those questions throughout the last months, trying to explain new concepts such as Tokenomics or Bonding curve easily.

I hope this book will help you understand this revolution better and go all-in in this space. Web3 is a positive sum-game where we all have an interest in onboarding new people in the space.

Acknowledgement

Special thanks to Jenil Thakker for his thoughtful feedback before publishing this book and for the opportunity he gave me to live from my passion. Thank you, Ashish Kumar, for the cover of this book. Special thanks also to Héloïse Pajot for taking the time to read this book before anyone else, providing me with invaluable feedback, and making this book what it is today.

I would also like to thank my mother and siblings, my grandmother, Océane Carénou, Léo Tizot, Pierre Want, Hugo Tran, Julien Bortolato-Robin, Estelle Bujeat, and Chris Chaboya, for their invaluable support throughout the years. May all writers be surrounded by such supportive people.

I

Part One: Web3 basics

This part will explain the basic principles of Web3. It will introduce Social Tokens, explain the use-cases of this technology, and answer the most common questions around this virtual currency.

1

Chapter 1: Blockchain basics

From the many conversations I've had with my friends and people outside of the crypto world, this space looks scary. The term "Crypto" is too often associated with "scams" and "speculation," and it feels intimidating to jump into this space without any previous knowledge. And I felt the same.

However, with a full-time job in Crypto in the past months, I've discovered a whole ecosystem, a broad community of individuals driven by the same passion and playing in a positive-sum game. What felt scary at the beginning, going all-in into Crypto, feels today like the best decision I've ever made.

The fear of this space by the broad majority is today one of the most critical problems the crypto world (that we'll call Web3 in this book) is facing. It prevents new talented individuals from building what might be one of the most disruptive technology and slows down the massive adoption of a powerful tool that could revolutionize our daily lives.

This book aims to make Web3 more accessible to as many people as possible and explain what is now possible with this technology and how this works concretely. If, at the end of this book, the Web3 space feels a little bit less scary, and you might even want to give it a shot, I'll have succeeded, on my own scale, to help onboard the next millions of individuals.

It has been quite a challenge to know where to start this book, as Crypto is sprawling. You can't explain a concept without having to explain at least three others. To make sure you don't feel lost throughout this book, I've decided to start by explaining the Blockchain basics and what, concretely, is Crypto.

I'm non-technical, and you won't need to know how to code to understand this book. I'll try to use many metaphors and concrete examples to explain some technical aspects of this revolution.

While this book will be mainly focused on Social Tokens, on the concrete use-cases, what they can change in our daily life, and less focused on the technical aspect of Social Tokens, I think it's important to understand the basics of this technology and how it works. You'll also find a Crypto's Lexicon at the end of this book for further definitions of technical terms.

1 - Blockchain Basics

For a large majority of us, the differences between Crypto, Blockchains, and cryptocurrencies can be messy. But when you start digging into it, you quickly realize that this whole technology ecosystem is pretty understandable.

I think the most important thing to understand is what a Blockchain is. Basically, a Blockchain is a digital ledger leveraging cryptographic mechanisms to secure transactions. Whenever someone wants to do a transaction on a blockchain, instead of asking a third party to secure the transaction, anyone can ask directly to the network to secure the transaction.

Basically, the transaction sender sends a Cryptographic message to the network where individuals with powerful computers then try to decrypt this message. Once it is decrypted, the block is secured, and the transaction is added to the open ledger. The person that decrypted the message, called a "Miner," earns a "tip" on the transaction.

From a user perspective, it's not really different from the experience we're living on the current internet (Web2). When someone's buying an e-book on Amazon, for example, the user only has to click on the "purchase" button, and trust Amazon they will make sure the seller actually send the e-book. If the seller never sends the e-book, the buyer will take Amazon as responsible, and Amazon will have to reimburse the purchase.

On a Blockchain, instead of going to Amazon to purchase an item, someone can go on a decentralized marketplace, click on the "purchase" button, and wait until the transaction is secured.

But let's go further with this example of an e-book. To sell something on the blockchain, the first thing to do is put the item on it, the same way an author is publishing the e-book on Amazon. We're using the term "to mint" or "minting," the process of putting an item on a Blockchain. Then to purchase an e-book, the buyer will have to own some virtual currency, some of the most famous ones being Bitcoin and Ethereum.

With both elements of the transaction, the money and the e-book, now on the blockchain, miners can now execute the smart contract. This is only possible because, previously, other miners have validated the transaction when the seller put their book on the blockchain, and the buyer bought some virtual currencies via the blockchain.

Let's now dig more into the concept of Smart contract. A smart contract is a code that only accepts the transaction when all the conditions have been met. For our example, we could imagine a smart contract that would say, "if the seller has actually created (minted) the e-book, and the buyer has sufficient funds, then, and only then, the transaction will be accepted."

The whole concept of a blockchain is that everything is "on-chain" and easily accessible. A blockchain is an open ledger that anyone can access. Every time a transaction is taken, someone from the network has verified it. Anytime anyone receives money, sends money, or buys an item, someone secures the transaction and adds it to the open ledger. Instead of doing these verifications manually, some people from the network agree to put some of their computing power to decrypt the cryptographic messages and make the network more secure in exchange for a tip.

To go back to our Amazon example, to buy an e-book, you need sufficient funds in your bank account. Whenever you're buying something on Amazon, they send a request to your bank that assures you have sufficient funds on your account and then send you the e-book, adding another third party to the transaction. The same thing goes with decentralized platforms. Decentralized platforms need to ensure you have enough funds (cryptocurrencies) in your crypto-wallet (your crypto bank account). To do that, when creating an account on their platform, they ask you to connect your Crypto wallet. By linking your

Crypto-Wallet to their blockchain, they have the capabilities, again, as everything is on-chain, to verify you have sufficient funds. There's no need for a third party anymore; everything is secured by cryptographic mechanisms and accessible by anyone.

To summarize, a blockchain is the ground layer of everything. Miners are the people securing the transaction. A smart contract is a piece of code that will assure both parties have what's needed for the transaction and validate it only if all the conditions are met. A crypto-wallet serves as a way to prove your identity in Web3 and as a virtual wallet where you can store your cryptocurrencies.

If you're interested in learning more about Crypto's glossary, I've put together a full chapter at the end of this book with further terms used in Web3.

2 - Crypto Mechanisms

We'll often talk about "Crypto Mechanisms" throughout this book, and even though we've just seen how those crypto mechanisms work, I think it's essential to dig a bit more into it and showcase some use-cases.

The main interest of these Crypto mechanisms is to build trust between individuals that don't know each other.

One example of those "crypto mechanisms" is the "Multi-Signature Wallet." A Multi-Signature Wallet is a Crypto Wallet that allows you to manage your community crypto assets, with the option to require a predefined number of signatures to confirm transactions. As it is necessary to have multiple team members to ensure every transaction in order to execute it, it prevents unauthorized access to the fund in

7

this wallet. No one can leave with all the money as it would require the authorization of all the other members.

Another exciting example of what crypto mechanisms allow is that anyone can vote for future decisions, with voting power proportional to the number of Tokens they have. For example, Snapshot is a decentralized voting system leveraging the capabilities of Social Tokens that provides flexibility on how voting power is calculated for a vote. Snapshot supports various voting types to cater to the needs of organizations. As it is decentralized and linked to your crypto wallet, the process of voting for critical decisions is easy, even though the different parties do not know each other or are in different regions of the world.

*

While I think it's essential to understand Crypto's basics, the long-term goal is to allow anyone leveraging this technology without knowing how this works properly and provide a better user experience than today. You don't need to understand how HTTP or TCP-IP protocols work to search on the internet today. The goal is that more people will surf on the decentralized Web without knowing too much of the technical aspects.

With this understanding of Blockchain basics, we can jump more into what excites me the most about the Web3 space: Social Tokens.

2

Chapter 2: Introduction to Social Tokens

Since last year, we've seen the NFT space booming. NFT stands for Non-Fungible Token and are unique digital tokens stored on a blockchain, meaning it's impossible to have two times the exact same one. Mainstream media covered some of the most significant NFTs sales, and so far, in 2021, NFT sales have totaled more than $13 billion.

Some 500 Fortune have entered this space, such as Budweiser, who purchased the domain name "Beer.eth", VISA, which bought an NFT, and Arizona Ice Tea, which purchased an NFT from one of the most famous collections to date. I'm sure you've even heard some people that aren't tech-savvy talking about NFTs. It seems like they are everywhere.

This space is so trending that, OpenSea, the leading NFT marketplace, surpassed, in August 2021 alone, the last quarter gross merchandise volume of Etsy ($3.04 billion).

Thanks to this hype, more people are becoming familiar with crypto in general and have created a wallet. The Crypto wallet platform MetaMask sees user count surge 1,800% in a year to top 10 million in august 2021.

Crypto is slowly becoming mainstream.

However, some people still don't get the point of NFTs. Why would someone want to buy one of these? Today, NFTs often have to do with status, scarcity, and belonging. While it's already a giant step forward in ownership and better revenue-sharing, NFTs still seem meaningless to a large audience.

In the latest months, we saw a new trend emerge that provides more utilities than NFTs: Social Tokens. Some of the world's biggest creators, celebrities such as Lil Yachty or Akon, have already launched their Token.

So what exactly is a Social Token? Has it the potential to revolutionize how people are collaborating? Is now a good time to jump into this revolution? That's what we're going to explore in this chapter.

1 - What are social tokens?

Put simply, social tokens are a way to incentivize anyone to work toward joint projects in a DAO, a crypto-based decentralized community, in exchange for a digital currency. This digital currency can then be redeemed in exchange for other cryptocurrencies or special perks within the community the token is associated with, such as access to token-gated content, the right to vote on future strategic decisions, or early access to community NFTs.

DAOs are firstly virtual places where people passionate about the same things decide to join forces to hang out and achieve high-ambition goals. It's not about work. It's first and foremost about culture, about vibing together and creating what you've always wanted to create. In DAOs, culture comes first, products and projects come second. There are many types of DAOs, some focused on building products for the crypto world and some focused on social networking. All DAOs, even socially-focused ones, are building different products with different ways to organize their work, and social tokens are how they can accomplish these goals.

Social tokens are cryptocurrencies like any other regular cryptocurrency. But the benefit of creating a social token is to give community leaders the power over the distribution of the token.

The goal of creating a social token is to build a virtual economy where early believers and contributors can share the upsides. Contributors who help the community grow by contributing to the different projects the DAO is building are given shares, or social tokens, with the aim of creating such an ambitious and robust community and projects that people are keen to buy the token to gain access to membership-only content, perks, and voting power in the community. Instead of simply getting paid with an existing cryptocurrency (similar to a salary), contributors are incentivized to help the organization succeed, as the value of their tokens — directly correlated to the success of the project — can gain an almost infinite value. Think of it like receiving equity as an early employee of a startup.

Social tokens also allow community leaders to reward contributors fairly. Unlike a startup, you don't need to be one of the first contributors to have a decent amount of your community's token. Even if you join at a later stage, you'll be rewarded for your work. It's a much fairer distribution of power than traditional startup models.

On top of the advantages that social tokens provide within a decentralized community, they are also easily tradable. Token holders don't have to wait until someone wants to buy their tokens to sell them; they can simply exchange them for another cryptocurrency at any time, which makes their value less hypothetical than an NFT's.

Finally, there's no need to get capital to jump into the social token revolution. There is no barrier to entry. Anyone can put in some work and invest their time in an online community and be rewarded with social tokens. After all, those who invest their time are the ones creating the real value for an organization.

2 - Social tokens as a way to create trust

The point of creating a social token is to incentivize collaboration by making it easy to collaborate with individuals that you don't know and that you don't specifically trust. Instead of setting up contracts and legal status to cover each contributor at the beginning, social tokens enable transactions on a blockchain, meaning there is an irrefutable record of the exchange.

Social tokens won't completely replace what we use now to create trust at work, such as legal contracts or regular, fiat payments, but they are a way to start small-scale projects more quickly.

One way tokens can do this is via a "multi-signature wallet." This wallet is a crypto wallet that allows you to manage your community crypto assets with the option to require a pre-defined number of signatures to confirm transactions. That way, no one can abandon a project with all the money that has been contributed since it would require the authorization of all the other members.

Crypto mechanisms also allow members to equitably vote on future decisions, with voting power proportional to the number of tokens a member has.

3 - What kind of organizations should use social tokens?

More than the tokens themselves, it's the ecosystem around them that is valuable — the community or organization. While NFTs are mostly speculative today and serve primarily as a way to show status and belong to a community, social tokens allow people to participate in these communities, build great things together and share the upsides.

Getting an NFT is like being an investor in a company, whereas getting social tokens in exchange for your work feels more like being an early employee. You'll be more involved, learn more, and have power over the community's future. It's much more fun than being an investor hoping for a return down the road.

Some projects have successfully leveraged the power of social tokens in recent months. For example, The Modern Billboard Collective is a project between three startups that aims to create a tokenized equivalent of the Million Dollar Homepage, a web page consisting of a million pixels arranged in a 1000x1000 pixel grid where anyone could buy a pixel for $1 and put an ad there, making the entire page worth $1 million. The collective aims to take this idea and, using tokens, allow brands to advertise without using a middleman on their respective websites by selling part of their homepage's pixels.

In the pursuit of leveraging crypto-mechanisms for the whole project, they also succeeded in creating trust between each of the three founding startups. Indeed, by letting anyone buy a digital "lot" on one of the three websites "on-chain," it is easy for each company involved in this collective to trust each other, as the royalties will be shared automatically and fairly between all of them. These experiments are made easy thanks to platforms like Coinvise that allow anyone to create a social token in minutes.

4 - Current state of Social Token space

As mentioned above, Social Tokens allow building ambitious projects that require strong collaboration to be achieved. Some decentralized communities have made a bet a few months/years ago to leverage the power of social tokens to incentivize cooperation, and many of these Web3 communities are currently thriving.

I can think of Friends With Benefits (FWB), a community full of thinkers and creators interested in Web3. FWB is similar to a social network, a space that has value because of the content and ideas the users of that social network create and share. This community has been growing tremendously in the past months and gathers more than 2000 community members, that all have paid their entry to this community for 75 $FWB. It's worth ~$8500 at the time I'm writing this book.

We also recently saw the launch of the $AGLD Token, a virtual currency that lives within the Loot ecosystem. The loot project was created by Dom Hofmann, the co-founder of Vine. Loots are "Randomized adventurer gear generated and stored on-chain." Basically, it's a collection of NFTs that will live within an ecosystem built by the community. The NFTs are only the raw pieces, and it's now up to the community to create use-cases around that. What makes Loot different is the number and variety of projects that have spun up around it. With

$AGLD, the virtual currency of the Loot ecosystem, the Loot holders can collaborate easily and vote on future strategic decisions. Every person that grabbed a Loot received 10k $AGLD. Those 10k $AGLD were worth ~$74K a few days after the launch.

Finally, the platforms fueling this space are also thriving. Coinvise, which seems to be one of the most promising startups in this space, is lowering the barriers to entry to anyone wanting to launch a DAO or a personal Token. Coinvise allows individuals to create and manage their tokens thanks to easy-to-use tools. Think Stripe for online communities. They raised $2.5M in 2021 and plan to extend their team and release more essential features for Web3 communities.

*

In the last few years, crypto has become much more widely adopted and understood due to consumer-friendly experiences aimed to appeal to the next cohort of crypto adopters.

We're seeing this unbundling of traditional employment happening in front of our eyes, and DAOs, fueled by Social Tokens, seem to be a promising path to re-invent the way we work and collaborate.

The space is currently booming, and I won't be surprised to hear more about social tokens in mainstream media in the following months.

As shown in this chapter, Social Tokens can be the next revolution in crypto. It facilitates collaboration and provides an easy way to work on multiple ambitious projects simultaneously, giving token holders flexibility and autonomy.

We're already seeing several communities growing steadily and having the potential to become billion dollars communities. The space is developing fast, but everything still needs to be built, and there are many opportunities ahead for ambitious and motivated individuals.

It might be a once-in-a-lifetime opportunity to grow with these new Web3 communities and be rewarded for being part of this revolution. Throughout the next chapters, we will explore more broadly the possibilities of this technology and dig into the use-cases that Social Tokens finally unlock.

3

Chapter 3: The Creator Economy & DAOs

GenZ, the emergence of The Creator Economy, and Covid-19 have changed the status-quo of companies as we know them. Individuals worldwide crave more flexibility, autonomy, and companies still struggle to evolve quickly enough to keep up with all those changes.

Some of our friends or family have started new side-projects or have pursued their hobbies during the pandemic, and for some of them, it's now their dream to quit the traditional career path and live from their passion.

We're leaning toward a more fluid way of working. Individuals will follow their interests, collaborating on multiple projects simultaneously, without having the constraint of working at a company. We're seeing this unbundling of traditional employment happening in front of our eyes. As a society, we have to re-invent the way we work, interact socially, communicate, and ensure comfort and security at work.

1 - The rise of the Creator Economy

GenZ is the side hustle generation. They admire Youtubeurs that can live from their passion. They've found out they can create a meme page and sell it for a thousand dollars. They can resell clothes from famous brands and earn a couple of bucks.

From a young age, they realized they could hustle to make money online. According to a recent Nielsen study, about 54% of Gen Z indicated they wanted to start their own company. Gen Z is the most entrepreneurial generation to date, often defined as 'self-starters.'

GenZs are also creators. They post on the internet, share photos, join forums, and curate articles. The internet levels the playing field, and anyone can use their hustle and savvy to amass a following and monetize that following. This is the creator economy.

But the Creator Economy and the term Creator is not only limited to GenZ. A creator is anyone pushing ideas, and a vision, through content on the internet. Jeff Kauffman Jr., for example, which might not be considered as a creator in a traditional sense, has created a thriving community around advertising and marketing in Web3. He's pushing his ideas and vision through essays and podcasts, gathering a strong community keen to help him achieve his high ambition goals. Dom Hofmann, the founder of Vine, is also a great example of this new wave of creators. Through his project Loot, Dom revolutionized how we're collaborating leveraging NFTs and has gathered a community that collaborates to achieve a large goal.

The Creator Economy results from a complete paradigm shift in the way individuals see the work. Many people don't want to work for others as they discovered they could make money on the internet by applying their skills in areas they love. They don't want to follow processes at a big corporation but rather collaborate on projects in which they thrive.

But there are still two major problems for creators today: Ownership and Collaboration. Since the appearance of the Creator Economy, we've seen three main phases for Creators on the internet :

- **From 00' to 10'** - Rise of social networking and User Generated Content platforms (TikTok, Instagram..). We saw the emergence of social media, which allowed everyone to have a voice on the internet and express their creativity through their content.
- **From 10' to 20'** - People who amassed an audience started to monetize. Creators, also called 'Influencers' at this time, discovered they could monetize their audience through those platforms and that it was possible to earn a living from their passion. They were helping others (brands & businesses) to achieve their goals.
- **From 20' to 30+'** - Creators will become their own business. Creators discovered they could now BE the brand, BE the product, and they could do for them what they were doing for others. Creators can now build a direct relationship with their 'fans' and create their ecosystem.

Creators need better infrastructure to join forces and accomplish high ambition goals. It's highly complex today for creators to collaborate as they don't have the right tools to do it, nor the experience.

To help creators perform in this 3rd phase, we need to give them the tools to collaborate easily with others.

2 - Creators DAOs - How Creators are building together

As Packy McCormick, a famous Web3 author, describes in his Coop-eration Economy article, we will see "liquid super teams, collections of individuals, each with their strengths, powers, and network, who combine forces to achieve goals". So, we'll see startups appear, right? Well, not really.

People started to create companies as it was easier to collaborate with someone in the long term. By hiring someone, you would assure that this person won't reveal the company's secrets, trust is created, and save cost on searching and onboarding new employees.

But over time, working for a company has shown limits. As a creator, accepting to work for a company for five years means saying no to hundreds of other exciting projects. You lose your flexibility as you have to work office hours, and you're not incentivized to do your best work as you have a monthly salary.

We're seeing this unbundling of traditional employment where the individual is now the atomic unit. Creators want to have the flexibility and the freedom to work on what they wish to, be their boss and work on projects that excite them. At the same time, those creators often need others to achieve their high ambition goals and don't want to work independently for the rest of their lives.

Working on a project with someone is all about trust. How can you ensure that this person you want to collaborate with is hardworking, reliable, and won't go out with the money? How do you put a group of highly talented individuals from all around the world that has never talked to each other together?

DAOs (short for Decentralized Autonomous Organizations) have emerged in recent years, allowing people to collaborate on smaller-scale projects than companies. DAOs are a new way to finance projects, govern communities, and share value. DAOs, compared to traditional companies, are open, global, and transparent.

DAOs are organized around a mission that coordinates through a shared set of rules enforced on a blockchain. DAOs are virtual places where people passionate about the same things decide to join forces to hang out and achieve high-ambition goals. Basically, a DAO is a group that leverages many of the new Web3 tools at their disposal and has decided to collaborate in a decentralized way, meaning with no proper hierarchy or top-down management. Social Tokens serve as virtual money for those DAOs.

In a sense DAO and Social Tokens could be compared to startup and equities.

But unlike traditional companies, thanks to cryptographic mechanisms, DAOs let people collaborate most easily and more efficiently together. Here are the benefits of DAOs:

- **Incentivize people in a more thoughtful way** - DAOs have the power to mint/issue/award tokens to their members that labor for the DAO. Tokens reward the most active users for their collaboration and motivate and incentivize people to participate and make sure the project will succeed. Indeed, by getting tokens of a project, you'll see its value growing over time if the project succeeds.
- **Share the benefits** - By creating a Token, a virtual currency for your DAO, you'll be able to reward contributors for their work. You'll be able to split the revenues in a more thoughtful way, where everyone will be rewarded in pro-rata of their contribution.

- **Allow better governance** - The fundamental difference between DAOs and companies is that it's the group of individuals who team up around missions and values that vote for their decisions. Its users vote on the proposals. The more tokens you have, the more voting power you have. It allows a genuinely flat culture and removes all hierarchy. Everyone can vote on future decisions in a truly equal way.

- **Increase productivity** - DAO's will establish a new paradigm in work culture, where individuals won't work from 9-5 and won't need to go to the office. People contributing to DAOs genuinely believe in the projects they are working on as they receive the DAO virtual currency, which has no inherent value. Working with passionate people changes everything.

- **Easier onboarding** - DAOs are using cryptographic mechanisms to enforce every action by a blockchain. Therefore, everything is on-chain, which means that everything is public and that you can prove the actions that have been taken in the past. It allows new ways of collaborating. For example, by enabling people to demonstrate their past experiences and their skills with on-chain credentials, hiring someone competent and HR won't have to guess if a candidate is skilled or not, nor base their choice on the reputation of the School of the candidate. It will also allow people to bring their reputation to new projects.

- **Provide more flexibility** - DAOs will also allow working on more flexible and small-scale projects. One of the reasons why you're creating a startup is for legal status. It's to make sure a contract binds together you and the people you're working with. But, in DAOs, smart contracts solved the trust problem. It won't make sense to create a startup if you want to work with other designers on a drop or a two weeks project, but it will make sense to create a DAO.

The Future of Work will be made of individuals seeking autonomy and meaning at work who want to collaborate to achieve great things, and DAOs seem to be the most promising path to achieve this vision.

In my opinion, it's under this more decentralized structure that the next big companies will be built because DAOs allow a much more efficient way to collaborate and align incentives.

*

The idea behind DAOs is that people don't need to be gig workers for someone else; they can find a group of people and build their own business together. Why would you want to work for others when you can be your boss and collaborate with friends around common values?

There will be fewer gatekeepers. Traditional economic and cultural institutions will have less influence and power. Work will continue to disaggregate, and the next generation of entrepreneurs will be "solopreneurs."

*

At this point, you should understand a bit more Crypto's key concepts, such as Social Tokens and DAOs. It's now time to explore further how, concretely, jump into this space. The next chapter will answer some of the most commonly asked questions around Social Tokens and how to go all-in this space.

4

Chapter 4: Jumping into this revolution

As seen in the previous chapter, Creators discovered they can now BE the brand, BE the product, and they could do for them what they were doing for others. These individuals, pushing their vision through content on the internet, can now build a direct relationship with their community and create their digital currency (Social Tokens) in their own economy.

1 - What to do with a Social Token?

Social tokens are best used when they scale or incentivize coordination and engagement between communities. Incentives are ideal when it's mutually beneficial to you and your community. You also have to understand that crypto and social tokens are still early, and we're only scratching the surface of what's possible. There are new exper-imentations with social tokens every week, and everyone's trying to push this space forward as we go.

Here are some use cases where creators could leverage their Social Token:

- **Allow their fans to invest in them early** - Having equity in an individual is much more than speculation. It's more about participation and how anyone can participate in helping grow and share the upside. It incentivizes people around a common goal. By believing in the creator early and helping them, community members will get a slice of their revenue once they've become more famous. The creator will get their help and some money to start in exchange for a portion of their future payments.
- **Create bounties to incentivize the community to help you grow** - Creators can ask their community to rate a podcast on Apple Podcast or write a review on Amazon in exchange for a certain amount of the $NAME token.
- **Crowdfund through an NFT** - Creators can create and sell an NFT such as a unique autographed book, a YouTube video, or a piece of art and use it to fund your future projects. Again, their community will get ownership over the project and will be incentivized to hype it up.
- **Create premium experiences** - By holding enough $NAME tokens, certain community members could have access to special perks such as the first chapters of a writer's next book in advance, access to a private Discord server, or redeem for one hour of their time, for example.

2 - Steps to follow to create a DAO

First, you have to understand that creating a Social Token for a decentralized community is not complicated, even for non-tech people. The difficulty is to get it accepted by the community. How do you foster a strong community around your project? How do you share your vision? You don't need Technical skills but social ones.

Indeed, culture is centric in DAOs. It's not about work. It's first and foremost about culture, about vibing together and creating, with others, what members have always wished to create. In DAOs, culture comes first, products and projects come second.

It's also important to clarify that there won't be one moment when you'll say, "that's it, I have created a DAO." Asking "when do have I a DAO?" is like asking "when do have I a Startup?". What differentiates an entrepreneurial or side-project from a startup? Is that the legal status? Is that when you make your first dollar? In a startup, you usually create a great product and then create a company around it, and there's a thin line between building a project and saying you're the founder of a startup. The same thing goes for DAOs. In DAOs, you first create a strong culture and build products that appeal to the community. But there's one moment you can say, "Ok, now I have a DAO."

A DAO can be compared to a startup. Many people are trying to create a DAO but with no idea of the DAO's mission and don't have a clear vision on why a DAO would be best for their project. It's like if someone would come to you and say, "I'm going to create a startup and need help with the treasury, but I haven't found a startup idea yet." It doesn't make much sense. By reading this book, you'll understand better the use-cases of DAOs and should be able to launch yours, or join one, more easily.

While there is no one path to create a DAO, tokenized communities are usually following similar steps. Communities and creators are usually :

- **Step 1:** Gathering a solid community around a project.
- **Step 2:** Learning about Tokenomics and how to design great incentives.

- **Step 3:** Creating a Crypto Wallet and buying your first ETH.
- **Step 4:** Creating a Personal / community Token and sending some tokens to early contributors.
- **Step 5:** Creating quests (missions) and using a platform such as Coinvise to automate the process.
- **Step 6:** Learning more about crowdfunding projects in Web3 then creating NFTs to raise money.
- **Step 7:** Setting up treasury management & governance, learning more about Social Token's Financial aspects, and pooling liquidity for your token.

*

While the goal of the first part of this book was to introduce the basics of Web3, such as Social Tokens and DAOs, the three other parts will focus on deep-diving key concepts to participate in this revolution. We will explore the Tokenomics of a project, how to crowdfund a project leveraging the Web3 tools, what a Liquidity Pool is, and much more.

At the end of this book, you should have a clear understanding of the Web3 ecosystem, understand the more important terms, and be able to create your DAO by following the different steps above. The way we are working and earning money is about to change forever, so let's learn how to leverage the new tools at our disposal to achieve financial freedom and live from our passions.

II

Part Two: Leverage Social Tokens

With a better understanding of Social Tokens use-cases, we'll now explore how to leverage this technology in the second part of this book. We'll try to understand what Tokenomics is, how to crowdfund a project through Social Tokens, and how to design great Incentives.

5

Chapter 5: How to attract high-quality talent for your DAO?

Creator DAOs are on the rise, and we're seeing more and more creators building tokenized communities. One of the first thing creators need to achieve their high-ambition goal is talent.

But it is not a small task to attract high-quality talents as there are hundreds of exciting projects going on. So how to attract those top talents to help you achieve broader goals?

Three mains parameters have shown their efficiency in previous DAO experiments: having a strong culture, a well-designed onboarding flow, and creating good incentives.

In this chapter, we will go through those three parameters and try to guide you on how to attract top talents to your DAO.

1 - Having a strong culture

Culture in a DAO is the most important asset you can hope for. Culture is the reason why high-quality talents will provide support over a sustained period for your DAO.

There's only so much you can motivate someone with financial rewards, but with a strong culture, community members will actively contribute, intrinsically motivated by the values you have and the desire to be assimilated with the project you're creating. High-quality talents are the ones who invest their time instead of capital, the ones who truly believe in the project and are keen to do whatever it takes to make it grow. Those are the most valuable and rarest contributors.

People in the Web3 space often display exclusive NFT avatars as their profile pictures and display such or such community in their Twitter bio. The reasons they are doing that are culture and social status. With a strong culture, people are keen to assimilate their personal brand with your community. Culture is the glue of crypto. Without culture (meaning, story, community, memes...), NFTs wouldn't cost such an astronomical amount. What people are buying when purchasing a high-value NFT is not really the piece in itself. They buy the right to be part of a broader project in which they truly believe and want to be assimilated. NFTs don't cost their price for their utility but for the social signal and the culture they have shaped around it.

When people are displaying in their Twitter bio that they are contributors to such a community, they signal that the DAO they are displaying has created a strong culture that has values and goals worth the time of the person. We're all "status-seeking monkeys," and we're always on the hunt for things to enhance our identities. The goal of a Creator

DAO is to create a culture so strong that people will promote it and work for it at a minimal cost, working mainly for the social value it provides. Members of a community share a piece of their identity. This collective identity is one of your most vital selling points.

Right, So how to create a strong culture?

- **Share a common vision** - Culture for every community is that one theme that people are aligned with, and that brings people together beyond your content. Any creator should seek this common thing, this right activity, which resonates with their audience and is better done as a group. This is how you create a strong culture. By creating a place where people with common interests can come and find their tribe, learn and grow together. Your goal as a community builder is to have community members engage with each other.
- **Know your community** - You need to understand your typical community member persona "deeply." As described by the interaction design foundation: *"Personas are fictional characters, which you create based upon your research to represent the different user types that might use your service, product, site, or brand similarly. Creating personas helps the designer to understand users' needs, experiences, behaviors, and goals."* In our case, by understanding what kind of profile you have in your community, it will be easier to design incentives, develop values, create specific group chats and find that common thing that speaks to your audience.
- **Have a clear mission and strong values** - The clearer you will be on what you want to achieve, and the values you have, the easier it will be to incentivize people to work with you. People will contribute in the long term only if they intrinsically believe in the project and gain social status by contributing.
- **Provide ownership** - You have to make the contributors feel

accountable for the success of the project and the culture. By giving ownership and by showing strong leadership (by actions and decisions), you'll not only make sure to attract the best talents, but you will also assure good retention of your best contributors.

- **Create trust** – Creating a strong culture is also creating trust. You need to build trust between members but also with people outside of the community. Having a public face behind the project has shown its efficiency to create trust. Hiring a scribe to facilitate the communication between team is also essential to create a healthy and sustainable trust culture.

To build a strong community, you have to find a "Why." It's all about having a common goal and a true belief. As a community leader, building a community with a strong culture is a long journey.

Building a strong culture is only the first step to attract quality talents to your DAO. With a strong culture, potential contributors will probably notice you and try to understand better what you're doing. Once in your community, the next step is to incentivize them to participate and help the DAO grow...

2 - Designing great incentives

The main interest of creating a Token for your community is to incentivize potential contributors to participate and give their time to make your project grow. There are three primary types of incentives:

- **Social Incentives** – It's more of a social, collectible value that people are proud to own. Think of airline miles that generate status within a specific sphere (airline lounge, first to enter the plane etc..). Likewise for special perks in Discord servers.

- **Vision Incentives** - members aren't participating "for-profit" (aka economic incentives) but are driven by a specific ideology. Community members will exchange your Token without a monetary value because they sincerely believed in the vision.
- **Economic Incentives** - it doesn't require a particular strategy, and you can simply ask community members to achieve a mission in exchange for economic value. By creating a pay-for-performance incentive scheme, anyone can provide their skills and help grow the project.

Well-designed incentives are essentials to attract quality talents for your DAO. Economic incentives are a great way to onboard new people to your project, but sustaining a community only based on financial incentives in the long term can be complicated. You should try to design bounties and rewards contributors that are here for the vision of the project and its social aspect, not for speculation. By giving ownership and rewarding high-quality talents with well-designed incentives, you'll make sure to create a sustainable and healthy community that can thrive in the long run.

Bounties and rewards can take many forms but should always fit into the broader goal of your community. A great example of an incentive that can be applied in almost all communities is a "Referral bounty." Leveraging its community to attract qualified people by rewarding existing contributors when they refer people they know has shown to be an efficient way to attract top talents in the past.

With a strong culture and effective incentives, you should already be able to attract high-quality members for your Creator DAO. However, to make sure those talents contribute actively and provide value, you'll need a well-design onboarding process.

3 - Having a well-design onboarding process

Being a member of a couple of DAOs myself, I've found it very time-consuming to browse the many channels of a Discord server and understand where I can provide value. There is a lot of confusion and plenty of non-relevant information to sift through, and it can be scary and demotivating for new potential contributors. To attract top talents, it's essential to make sure the onboarding process is straightforward. You should think about the user journey and create an onboarding process that makes it easy for anyone to participate.

An example of a great onboarding process could be BanklessDAO. Their Wiki is organized to participate even though you don't have much time to provide to the DAO. By doing that, they are making sure that no one feels intimidated and therefore are making sure to receive help from the maximum of people.

They also have clear documentation about the different guilds of the DAO and their respective missions, making it easy for anyone to see where they think they could provide the most value.

Finally, once you've identified the guild you could bring the most value to, they are making the process of contacting someone from this guild easy. It's still rare to see a well-designed onboarding process in DAOs today, and potential contributors often still have to send a direct message to one (or several) community leaders(s) and ask how they can provide value, making the whole process longer and less effective. By creating a well-designed onboarding process (clearly explaining what you need help for, what your DAO is doing, and making it easy for potential contributors to reach out to a qualified member), you'll have a competitive advantage compared to other DAOs.

*

Attracting quality talents for your DAO is not an easy task, but by making sure to have a strong culture, a well-designed onboarding process, and good incentives, you should be able to work with high-quality contributors and successfully grow your project. The most successful DAOs tend to lower entry barriers and combine a strong culture with a sense of ownership for every contributor. While attracting high-quality talent is not a small task, it might be even harder to retain them in an economy of abundance, where new exciting projects are being created every day.

6

Chapter 6: Retaining high-value talents to your DAO

In his essay "Growing a Tokenized Community," Louis Albiverse developed a framework called "The DAO Community Growth Cycle," where he argues that to grow a DAO, community leaders have to Attract, Recruit and finally Engage potential contributors. While this model is highly insightful, I think a fourth step is to add to this growth cycle: Retain. Indeed, Crypto is 100% an employee market today. There are more job offers than good candidates.

DAOs are unlike traditional companies. DAOs enable fluidity of collaboration and provide flexibility. But the fluid nature of DAOs also makes it hard to retain consistent talents that drive an important amount of impact on the DAO. Plus, this fluid nature of work comes with the risk that the most active contributors get frustrated by the level of engagement of the less active ones.

That's why today, contributor retention is one of the most critical metrics for a DAO, and one of the most pressing problems those new decentralized organizations have to tackle. Growth, scaling, and mass adoption will follow only if DAOs solve the current problem of contributors' engagement. By solving this problem, more DAOs will grow thanks to their long-term contributors, which will make their community more attractive to people outside of Crypto, attracting more new contributors and reinforcing this positive feedback loop.

The million-dollar question now is, how can DAO leaders retain the best contributors and create a community strong enough to keep them engaged in the long term? How can they leverage the new tools at their disposal to tackle this problem? How can the paradigm shift in the way individuals collaborate in DAOs be a strength, not a weakness?

This chapter will explore how Culture, Tools, and Ownership might be the perfect recipe for high retention in a DAO.

1 - What do contributors want?

Many researchers have conducted studies to investigate retention, productivity, and supportive cultures in traditional organizations in recent years. The key knowledge and models that organizational psychologists have developed can give great insight into the essentials of a great DAO.

While there are many ways to contribute positively to employee well-being, three specific elements seem to have a consistently strong influence over the retention of employees in an organization:

- **Culture** - The organization creates a strong culture and share a long-term vision and values with contributors.
- **Tools to succeed** - The organization provides contributors the tools they need and makes the collaboration easy.

- **Autonomy / ownership** - The organization gives enough flexibility to contributors along with ownership over the projects.

Let's dig more into each of these three elements.

1.1 - Tell me what is expected of me... (Culture)

Recent research from McKinsey shows two reasons why employees in traditional companies are leaving: a lack of sense of belonging at work (51%) and lack of feeling their work is valued by the organization (54%). In short, to retain employees, give them a sense of purpose and community.

And that's exactly what DAOs and the Web3 ecosystem can provide.

Traditional companies have, for long, tried to create a strong culture and foster belonging. But the primary purpose of a company, by definition, is to make a profit. Culture is often a second layer serving the purpose of making a profit and acquiring new market shares.

On the other end, DAOs are firstly virtual places where people passionate about the same things decide to join forces to hang out and achieve high-ambition goals. It's not about work. It's first and foremost about culture, about vibing together and creating, with others, what you've always wished to create. In DAOs, culture comes first, products and projects come second. Not the other way around.

Because of its intrinsic structure, because, by design, DAOs lack the traditional hierarchy of a physical organization, they've focused on providing support through the culture and the goals they maintain.

The most successful DAOs have all created a strong culture through 5 key elements (that we discussed in the previous chapter).

But creating a great culture is only the first element to better retention of employees. Without the right tools and enough flexibility, it won't be sufficient to retain active community members.

1.2 -And give me what I need to meet those expectations... (Tools to Succeed)

For contributors to keep working for a DAO, they need to have the right tools at their disposal to do great work.

Luckily, social tokens, the virtual currencies fueling DAOs, have the significant advantage of facilitating the coordination between contributors through a large set of tools. Indeed, many new tools allow community leaders to manage the daily needs of their contributors and leverage the power of Social Tokens to make the whole process easy and trustworthy.

Indeed, by leveraging crypto mechanisms, many actions can now be taken "on-chain," meaning secured on a blockchain, facilitating the whole process.

There is a large ecosystem of DAO tools, and to retain high-value community members, it seems essential to dig into them and implement those who make the most sense for your community.

Communication tools such as Discord, Telegram, or Geneva are essential. Indeed, Research by McKinsey suggests that town hall meetings and immersive, small-group sessions are effective at helping employees align their day-to-day work with the organization's broader mission.

DAOs have to face this problem of asynchronous communication even more than traditional companies. In DAOs, contributors are often spread out worldwide, and most of them don't work full-time for the DAO. To avoid this lack of communication, it's important to think thoroughly about the channels that need to be created in the Discord, set up weekly meetings, hire scribe responsible for taking notes at these meetings, etc...

Along with communication tools, because there is no strong hierarchy in DAOs, it's also essential to implement workflow tools. Indeed, in many DAOs today, there's a weird loop of DAO leaders wanting members to start initiatives, but members not knowing what makes sense to start for the community and then end up in an impasse. Without robust workflows, potential contributors will quickly be discouraged and end up not contributing at all.

To overcome this, it's essential to create guilds (or working groups) with accessible docs of what's needed within each guild. For a DAO to work, it needs weekly meetings, an easily accessible list of missions, easy access to a doc with the name of the contributors from the guild (with a person to contact in case of a problem) etc... Most DAOs are still using the Google suite (created for Web2 use-cases), and there is room for improvement in this space.

DAO leaders can also set up tools to boost employees' sense of confidence or to encourage gestures of kindness and support, two critical elements for contributors' well-being at work. For example, this can be achieved by allowing anyone to send tips to other contributors through the Discord bot Collab.land.

1.3 - And then leave me to it... (Autonomy/ flexibility/ownership)

Lastly, a DAO must provide autonomy and flexibility to retain its contributors with the right tools and a great culture.

Few people enjoy unwarranted scrutiny, and plenty of research supports the positive outcomes that autonomy inspires. Autonomy relates to feelings of voice and control. DAOs are fluid by nature and provide ownership and a lot of independence.

The flexibility that DAOs offer is also a great advantage as DAO leaders can provide contributors with the flexibility to work only on the tasks they like. Contributors can work on a project and leave. The goal is not to involve them in every project but to have a strong enough culture and workflows to make them come back.

The downside of the DAOs structure is that, with no proper hierarchy, contributors have to put some work into the project without receiving specific orders but delivering on time because they believe in the long-term goal and are immersed in the culture.

There's a thin line between allowing too much flexibility and not enough, and this line can vary between DAOs, depending on their contributors and culture.

With flexibility should also come ownership. The core team should give ownership over the projects to contributors by letting them vote on important decisions and future missions, and ownership over the company by allowing contributors to invest in the DAO and have shares in it. Aligning incentives is everything in Web3.

Lastly, I would encourage DAO leaders to overcompensate their contributors with their native token. With tokens come ownership and skin in the game. By doing so, DAO leaders will bootstrap contributor retention with more significant ownership stakes and scale back when it's time.

2 - Structural Models

On top of all those good managerial practices, that allow to Attract, Recruit and finally Engage, some good structural models can also be put in place to retain contributors. In the second part of this chapter, we'll explore the two main models and how they can help DAO leaders.

2.1 - The reward model (PUSH MODEL)

The reward model aims to push advantages and rewards to contributors to convince them to stay.

One great example of this model is what the Nouns DAO is doing. Nouns are an experimental attempt to improve the formation of on-chain avatar communities. There's a new noun every day (a new avatar as an NFT), and you need to win the auction to get it.

Because 100% of noun auction proceeds are sent to Nouns DAO, Nounders (project's founders) have chosen to compensate themselves with nouns. Every 10th noun for the first five years of the project (noun ids #0, #10, #20, #30, and so on) will be automatically sent to the Founder's multisignature Wallet to be vested (we'll come to the concept of vesting later in this book), and shared among the founding members of the project (which represents 10% of supply for first five years). This incentivizes the founders of Nouns to work on this project as a long-term initiative.

This model also provides long-term contributors stability, which is a great advantage in an uncertain space like Web3.

Another great example is what the Forefront leaders have done. Through a Liquidity Mining Program, they've allowed their core contributors to invest in the DAO, with a vesting period of 1 year, which means contributors can't withdraw their money before one year. By doing so, they incentivize their contributors (now investors) to work hard and make the project grow.

One last example of this model is what the Global Coin Research community is doing. The community is divided into three tiers (Pioneer - Alpha - Gold), with the minimum of Token to access each tier increasing. Every month, they reward their members proportionally to their tiers, incentivizing them to be gold members and hold their Token for the long term.

This structural model is also good to increase the speed to ownership, meaning "how quickly can you put a meaningful amount of tokens in the hands of high-value contributors." With this model, DAO leaders also increase the ownership of their contributors and decentralize their community a bit more.

As Jess from Seedclub said: The scarce resource in web3 is Talent. Ownership is a competitive advantage.

2.2 - The membership model (PULL MODEL)

On the Pull model, instead of giving out rewards to incentivize people to stay, you incentivize the community members to become contributors and put in some work to make the DAO grow.

That's the model the Friends With Benefits (FWB) community has chosen. They have put a Membership in place to access their community. Membership focuses on the community's longevity and health, ensuring FWB remains a place we all continue to call home. Each season, they increase the minimum number of tokens someone should have to access the community, creating a new incentive for members to engage with a team of their choice, become a contributor, and be rewarded in Token for their work.

Some other models and initiatives need to be explored. For example, I haven't seen any DAO keeping some grants for long-term members. A portion of the treasury is allocated to the long-term onboarded members, not part of the core team. Another good way to ensure retention is also to pay the contributors higher than the market price. That's what Cabin DAO is doing, paying more than standard market rates where possible because they're in a high-risk environment. If your token payouts have high volatility, the pay should be much higher than a FAANG basic salary.

*

Packy McCormick, a famous Web3 author, explains in one of his essay that "Human mixing" is one of the four components of a Scenius. As he argues: *"If past clusters of genius were all local commercial trading centers, the internet is the world's trading center. It's hard to overstate or even understand the impact of pulling people from around the globe onto one big playing field."*

And I would go even further. We can't underestimate the impact of pulling people from around the world to work together in a completely new way, facilitated by a set of new tools and social tokens. DAOs have the potential to change the world by facilitating collaboration and accelerating innovation. But this bright future will only be possible if those DAOs can retain their high-quality talent in the long term.

To retain these high quality talents, it's essential to put in place the managerial and structural elements that we've explored in this chapter and continue to explore new good practices applied directly to this new way of collaborating.

Attracting and retaining high-quality talents is the first step in building a thriving community. The second is to incentivize these talents to put some work and help you grow the community.

7

Chapter 7: Designing great incentives

Incentives are ideal when it's mutually beneficial to you and your community. This will create positive-sum games, where everyone has an aligned economic interest. By designing great incentives, you'll reach a point where you'll have the power to gather a strong community keen to help you achieve broader goals and collaborate with others. This chapter aims to give you a framework to help you foster a strong group of contributors toward a joint project. When incentives are aligned correctly, they will push the solution to grow indefinitely.

1 - Understanding the different types of incentives

1.1 - Social incentives

First of all, you have to understand that a Social Token used purely for its utility can thrive in a niche community even though it has no monetary value. It's more of a social, collectible value that people are proud to own. Social Tokens create status within a community. Think of Airline miles that generate status within a specific sphere (Airline lounge, first to enter the plane, etc..) or special perks in Discord servers such as Discord roles, special reaction emoji, access to certain parts of the server etc. In the end, money is what people say is valuable. As Hyman Minsky said: "Everyone can create money. The problem is to get it accepted". So suppose you can provide something worthwhile within the community but has no monetary value (in our case – Social Status) through your Social Tokens. In that case, community members will be keen to exchange their time against this other valuable resource.

A great example is what the artist RAC did with his $RAC Token. Uniquely, fans can't *buy* $RAC; they can only earn it (by buying merch, supporting him on Patreon, achieving small tasks, etc..). By holding $RAC, fans can get access to a private Discord server, as well as early access to future merch drops. $RAC holders have a way to prove they are part of the 1% biggest fan. Social Tokens can reinforce the hierarchy within the community, incentivizing anyone to participate within the community to increase their social status.

Any niche will thrive because they have super fans who want to be part of a community and seek social status. Status symbols within communities are crucial for devoted fans. Think about the Star Wars fans willing to spend thousands of dollars for merchandise. Imagine now how big a project could become by letting those fans gain status through Social Tokens by helping grow this project. You can't underestimate the power of Social incentives.

1.2 - Vision Incentives

Many significant communities have succeeded even though the inter-ests of their members weren't "for-profit" (aka economic incentives) and were more driven by a specific ideology. We can think of the Bankless community, for example, where "members seek liberation from the tyranny of the traditional financial system" and where they "will achieve financial self-sovereignty, security, and prosperity." To achieve this great vision, collaboration is critical, and it firstly suited people who believed in the core ideology driving it. The movement has its currency, the $BANK, that has no financial value and simply represents participation in the bankless community. There is no sale. There are no investors. Community members will exchange this token without a monetary value because they sincerely believed in the vision.

Aligning interests is all about creating a token with embedded interest alignment for all parties who will use your token. Vision incentives can be powerful for broad and long-term projects, but it can, however, be complicated to motivate people in the short term.

1.3 - Economic Incentives

Economic incentives are the most straightforward incentives to put in place. Indeed it doesn't require a particular strategy, and you can simply ask community members to achieve a mission in exchange for economic value. By creating a pay-for-performance incentive scheme, anyone can provide their skills and help grow the project. It's clear what they will get in return. Creating Grant programs has also shown its efficiency to incentivize contributors participating in the project. With decentralized governance, anyone can submit a proposal (describing the missions, timeline, salary...) and get it accepted by the community.

It's also interesting to reflect on how to shape those grant programs. Do you reward only people who opt-in to a program (which forces them to be active but results in fewer people ultimately enrolled), or is it better to enroll everyone by default(which means better coverage, but users might be more passive)? Do you prefer to create schemes that enforce rigid hierarchies (Token-gated communities or channels for example, where there's a hierarchy between those with enough tokens and the other) or create flat-rate systems where everyone on the scheme has the same chance of getting a discount (by curating article for a community for example)? As an example, we can think of Collab.Land, which built a Discord bot, connected to an Ethereum wallet to verify token balance before joining a chat group. This allowed the creation of token-permission groups, such as $JAMM and $KARMA, which helped ensure that those joining the group had a certain level of skin in the game.

Economic incentives are a great way to onboard new people to your project, but sustaining a community only based on financial incentives in the long term can be complicated.

To create incentives that impact and boost a community sustainably and positively, you have to make sure your incentives are part of at least one of the three categories: Social, Vision, or Financial. In creating incentives that don't fit in those categories, you have a higher risk of seeing users not be motivated enough to engage in activities that increase the value of the community.

2 - The "Great incentives" Framework

Now that we've understood the different types of incentives, we'll try to develop a framework that can help any community leader design great incentives.

2.1 - Determine what would drive each party to use your token.

Everyone first chases personal interests. It's human. The aim of creating a Social Token is to align those interests with the ones of your community. Suppose you can make incentive mechanisms that align both the community interests and the personal interests of each community member. In that case, you'll foster a strong community willing to build a joint project. The first step to do so is to clearly define what members of your community are chasing by joining your community. What are their inner motivations? What would they earn by participating in the community? Why have they decided to join? You have to deeply understand their interest in collaborating with the community before creating incentives.

The second thing you should do, as a community leader, is to define the things you would need help with to achieve your mission. What are the activities that drive value for your community? Are you a curation community and looking for help to stay relevant? Are you a community aiming to share best practices and need everyone to be involved and share their skills?

2.2 - Determine how you can align each parties' interest.

Now that you know what you need and what other community members want, your goal is to align those interests and design targeted rewards schemes. University course grades, for example, provide powerful incentives for students to study hard or even to cheat, all without the university or the course instructor giving the student a dime. With grades, universities achieve their education goals while students are rewarded with good grades for their hard work. Designing great incentives, it's all about considering the trade-offs, which balance costs and benefits.

To align each parties' interest, you have to create incentives that provide sufficient value to your community to trade off their time. Students know that they can have good grades by spending hours learning their courses, and good grades can let them enter a good school and potentially have their dream job. They are trading their time against a potentially brighter future.

2.3 - Prevent bad token behaviors by disincentivizing those

When creating a Token for your community, you also have to think about the bad behaviors that could happen. Some bad behaviors could be speculative investments, for example, where community members would buy your token (try to raise its value) without having a positive impact on the project's value or development.

One way to beat this is to provide lock-up periods for token-holders. You reward token holders for holding your token, which disincentives them to sell and buy often and speculate.

Creating trust and having clear values can be sufficient to prevent your community from those bad behaviors, but it's good to keep in mind that those bad behaviors can occur and determine in advance the actions you could take to disincentivize them.

2.4 - Incorporating effective performance metrics and optimizing the size of rewards

To reward contributors efficiently, you also have to be clear about the quality of the work they are providing and, therefore, put in place clear performance metrics. The goal of defining clear performance metrics is to measure participants' contributions to reward them relative to their efforts.

Blockchain and smart contracts now allow easy measuring of those metrics. Indeed, tools like SourceCred allow community leaders to measure and reward value creation thanks to a Discord Bot. For example, thanks to SourceCred, it's easy to see the number of messages someone has sent in a Discord or if he has recently submitted work.

Creating good performance metrics is crucial to well-designed incentives. For example, token price is a poor performance metric for incentivizing the types of behaviors that blockchain platforms want their participants to engage in, and you should focus more on finding metrics that can measure the "quality" of the work done.

By following those four steps, you should be on the right track to well-designed incentives for your community. This framework aims not to give you a clear path to follow as there are no one-size-fits-all solutions. With this framework, you should ask yourself the right questions and decide for your specific use cases and your specific community. There are, however, some general pieces of advice that can be applied in pretty much every community.

- **Create a token only if you have at least three "realistic" token use cases** - From previous experiences, creating a token for your community with less than three realistic use cases makes it more likely to fail.

- **Start with short-term incentives** - Even though you have a long-term vision, it's essential to break it into smaller blocks and define specific missions that can be achieved in few hours.
- **Don't underestimate the power of game design for your incentives** - People will trade-off their time if you're asking them in a fun and gamified way.
- **Build trust & give ownership** - It's a long-term game to build trust, but it's essential to show your interest in every community member, always do the extra step, answer possible questions and give them ownership. By doing so, you'll create deep relationships with some members that will, in exchange, help you build a stronger community.

*

Crypto and Social Tokens finally allow easier collaboration. What was impossible only a few years ago is now a reality, and there are some super exciting niches out there that can be bound up with their own social money. In the end, everything will be tokenized as tokenization changes the equation. Any niche will thrive because they have super fans who want to be part of a community, part of a broader project. Those communities will need Social Tokens and great incentives to create better collaboration. Through Social Tokens, these tokenized communities will also have new tools at their disposal to crowdfund their project.

8

Chapter 8: Crowdfunding projects through Social Tokens

For the past years, the market of social tokens has been correlated to the broader Crypto market. But recently, we've seen this correlation diminish. Indeed, as creators understand more the use cases and the utilities of Social Tokens, they bring in more fans from outside of Crypto.

While the use cases of Social Tokens are numerous, one of the use cases that stood out in the latest months is Crowdfunding through the community. Indeed, we've seen many exciting projects leverage the power of Social Tokens to raise money and achieve their goals. Many new possibilities have been made possible thanks to Social tokens and Web3, and Creators are at the forefront of this revolution, leveraging those new technologies to crowdfund their projects and achieve their goals.

This chapter will explore the advantages of crowdfunding a project leveraging social tokens, understand the differences between crowdfunding on Web2 vs. Web3 for communities, and highlight the use cases with concrete examples.

1 - What does that exactly mean to crowdfund a project through social tokens?

In Web2 (centralized Web), creators asked their community to give USD to crowdfund a project. In Web3 (decentralized Web) the mechanisms are a bit different. Creators can mint (create) a social token (their personal digital currency) and use it the way they want. Creating a social token makes it easier for creators to raise funds as contributors will receive Social Tokens in exchange for their USD. Contributors are part of the project. They own a piece of it.

Let's say a videographer needs to get better video equipment and hire an editor. There weren't many possibilities for the Creator before social tokens to crowdfund its project through its community. It was complicated to manage the legal part, deal with the logistic, and rely on a centralized platform. With this new money, the videographer's fans can redeem a slice of it in exchange for USD. They will have access to unique experiences while helping the Creator achieve its goals. While the videographer would have asked in Web2 to its community to "support" his project, he can now in Web3 ask them to be part of it, giving them personalized exchange experiences, a slice of its future income, etc.. The community now has the power to invest in creators to crowdfunding and shape the project's future rather than simply supporting the project from an external position.

In the end, Creators are leveraging new technologies to involve their community in their projects while raising funds to achieve broader goals. That's how powerful Web3 can be.

2 - Why is it great to crowdfund through Social Tokens?

What if you've invested in Taylor Swift early, helping her buy her first studio sessions in exchange for a slice of her future revenues? Chances are, this small investment would have turned in a multi-thousand dollar profit today. Social tokens allow to not simply support an artist but be part of its journey and serve as a way to align incentives. Indeed, by having a share of Taylor Swift's future revenues, its community is incentivized to help her grow and promote her art.

The possibilities are endless for creators. Singers are now able to crowdfund their first album, writers their first book, and filmmakers their first film. By giving communities and fans ownership over the content and, therefore, by aligning incentives, we'll see more and more projects succeed, all thanks to the power of the community and social tokens.

As mentioned previously, crowdfunding a project through Social Tokens (Web3) is very different from doing it through traditional Web2 platforms. There are fundamental advantages to using social tokens to crowdfund your projects, mainly related to three aspects: financial, social aspect & governance aspect.

Let's dig more into the advantages of using social tokens to raise funds.

2.1 - Financial aspect

2.1.1 - *For Creators:*

- It allows Creators to raise money for their projects while aligning their upside with key stakeholders.

- Creators don't need to use the "all-or-nothing model", in which the money is only passed to project creators when the project reaches its established funding goal.
- Overcome the challenges of fundraising through traditional financing methods, which is often complicated for non-well-known projects.

2.1.2 - *For Community members :*

- They can buy and trade their tokens without any intermediary taking a cut on each transaction.
- It gives supporters of the project ownership over it. They won't simply support the project. They'll possess a piece of it, which means having economic incentives to help the project succeed.

2.2 - Social aspect

2.2.1 - *For Creators:*

- Incentivize fans to engage and promote the Creator's content. Community members have economic & Social incentives to help the project succeed.
- Creators have access to the skills of a whole community keen to help grow the project.

2.2.2 - *For community members:*

- Be a proud holder of $NAME tokens. Community members will have tokens in their Crypto wallet to prove they were there since the beginning and prove that they helped grow. They'll also have access to special perks and experiences.

2.3 - Governance & Decisions

2.3.1 - For Creators:

- Creators have control over the means and the production of their content throughout the process. It enables them to **maintain their creative vision.**
- Everything is decentralized, which means they don't need to ask permission from anyone to crowdfund, and platforms can't ban them. Web3 encourages collaboration and opens access to anyone wanting to build and share the upside without relying on centralized platforms anymore.

2.3.2 - For Community members:

- Give stakeholders (Community members) the chance to have a voice and influence the project's future. It reinvents the process of creating entirely. Fans can now actively participate in the project, and the biggest fans can pay more to have premium experiences and decision power. It allows creators to granular their pricing while giving the biggest fans the possibility to be part of the creative journey.

You should now clearly see the advantages of creating a Social Token to raise funds for a project instead of crowdfunding it through Web2 platforms. Many exciting projects have already leveraged this new technology to achieve their goals. We're going to explore those examples to better understand why Social Tokens were the best solutions for their use-cases.

3 - Examples of successful Social Token crowdfunding.

Let's dig more into examples of projects that successfully leveraged Social Tokens to crowdfund their project through their community.

- **Ethereum: The Infinite Garden - $INFINITE** - ETHEREUM: THE INFINITE GARDEN is a character-driven documentary film on the challenges and rewards of building a new world. The team exceeded their funding goal of 750ETH and raised 1035ETH(~$2.7M when I'm writing these lines). As the team behind the movie explain on their crowdfunding page: "as experienced, independent filmmakers, we understand the challenges of fundraising through traditional film financing methods." Social tokens have allowed the team to ask their community directly, without asking permission from anyone. They will enable them to maintain their creative vision of the film while ramping up production quickly to capture this evolving story in real-time. Furthermore, it allows them to involve the community in making the film by giving them access to the film's private Discord chat and credit them in the film.
- Project funded announcement
- **Burn Alpha Novel - $NOVEL** - As Emily Segal, the author of the Burn Alpha Novel says: "Usually, novelists go to great lengths to fund their own novel-writing process by working other gigs, selling commercial writing, or – in significantly fewer cases – getting an advance from a publishing company. All of these methods have drawbacks in the form of limited time or limited creative freedom for the author. On top of that, the process of creating these works of art goes on behind a veil of secrecy, away from the community that will ultimately enjoy the final product." She has decided to change that and crowdfunded her project through Social Tokens. By helping her achieve her goal to write a novel, contributors will

have a mention in the book's acknowledgments, access to periodic supporter-only readings of the manuscript in process, and one-on-one calls with her to chat about writing or whatever is on their mind. Social Tokens helped Emily unlock new experiences with fans while giving her more freedom over her content.

· **Alex Masmej - $ALEX** - Alex Masmej has created the $ALEX token and has decided to sell 10% of the $ALEX token supply against $20,000, claiming to give some of his future income for the next three years. As a 23 years old from France, Alex wouldn't have been able to do it without Social Tokens as it would have been a legal and logistical mess. He achieved his goal to raise $20K and has been able to move to San Francisco with this money. Alex is now the Co-Founder of Showtime, a platform that allows Creators and Collectors to showcase and Collect digital art, and an early investor in Coinvise.

· **Elektra by Songcamp - $ELEKTRA** - Songcamp Elektra is made up of 42 musicians, visual artists, developers and strategists. Together, they are building "Elektra" — an interactive choose-your-own-adventure web3 game with music at its core. As this project evolves, the lines between Creator and audience will blur. Game builders will play the game they are building, and game players will build the game they are playing. The funds raised through this crowdfunding campaign go entirely towards bringing this project to life. The project raised 80k thanks to newly wealthy crypto-natives reinvesting in the next generation of creatives on the internet. This kind of project would have had a hard time being funded through the classic path and would have lost total control over the project.

· **Creator Cabin - $CABIN** - The Creator Cabin DAO has built a new cabin designed as a collaborative co-living and working space for independent online creators. Their goal is to find ways to sustainably fund independent online creators and develop DAO-based governance models for physical spaces. Thanks to Social Tokens, they've crowdfunded their projects, and they collected $42k to experiment with their idea. It's an experiment in universal creator income, tech stacks for decentralized cities, and the physical manifestation of DAOs that has been made possible thanks to their community.

*

Crypto and Social Tokens allowed revolutionizing the fundraising processes. It will enable more projects to come to life, rewarding community leaders and community members to collaborate. With the funds in the treasury, community leaders will then have to figure out all the things that enable participants to contribute positively to the DAO.

9

Chapter 9: Tokenomics - building a tokenized community

With the creator economy booming, we're seeing more talented individuals sharing content online and gathering tight-knit tokenized communities.

As shown in the first part of this book, creating a Social Token is the easy part. What's more complicated is to get it accepted by a community. How will creators convince anyone to work for them in exchange of a virtual currency they just created? What actions can creators take to start a virtual economy with a digital currency being accepted by their whole community?

The answer is: having strong Token economics for their project. We call Tokenomics (Token + Economics) all the things that enable participants to contributing positively enabled by strong token design. Setting up Tokenomics for a project means "What can a creator put in place to allocate & incentivize a community to participate in the project."

Social tokens have shown their efficiency on incentivizing individuals to share their skills with others. Projects that have succeeded in creating thriving communities all have strong Tokenomics. Tokenomics is a successful community's superpower.

But setting up Tokenomics is not a small task for creators, specifically for those new to the crypto world. How many tokens should a creator allocate to contributors? How much of the supply should be reserved for the community's treasury? What will be the total initial supply? Many questions come to mind, and it's not always easy to have the correct answers.

In this chapter, we'll explore further what creators can put in place to create strong Tokenomics around their project, and aims to break it down into an easy-to-read step-by-step guide.

0 - Before starting

Before deep diving into Tokenomics, it's important to clarify certain things.

Creators should gather a strong community toward a joint project. A project beyond the creator themselves, a project that requires strong collaboration to be achieved. A singer can gather a large audience, but to turn this audience into a community, they need to have a broader project that requires collaboration. We could think of an album. Any fan could become a contributor by creating designs/posters, spreading the word, organizing crowdfunding and so on. We could also think of a fitness instructor making videos on Youtube, creating the go-to-place for everything related to having a healthy lifestyle. Fans, led by the creator, could create a platform, create challenges, and gather resources to achieve this broader goal. The point is: the project needs to go beyond the creator.

It's also important to clarify what a creator is. We will consider a creator as anyone pushing ideas, and a vision, through content on the internet.

Now, with a common definition of what we'll call a creator, and the prerequisites to create a thriving decentralized community, let's dig into the three main aspects of Tokenomics: Token design -Token Distribution -Financial aspects.

1 - Token design: What key factors should Creators take into account before creating the Token?

Token design is a critical component of creating a thriving community. It's essential as the Token design (aka - all the technical aspects of the token) will serve as a foundation to incentivize a community to participate in the project.

The first question that should come to mind when creating a Token should be "What will be the total initial supply?" or, in other words, "How many tokens should I create?"

There isn't a one-size-fits-all answer to "How much token should I create," but we'll go over the main characteristics that you should take into account to come up with an answer.

First of all, when creating a Token, there are two models, with both pros/cons, that you should be aware of.

- *The Fixed supply model* - It's a model where you define the number of tokens you want to create beforehand (for example, 10M tokens)

66

and receive them directly on a wallet.

· **_The Bonding curve model_** – Anyone has to buy the Token to create it. Its price increases as the Supply or distribution of the Token do. The more tokens have been distributed, the higher the price. Let's take an example to illustrate what a bonding curve is. You've just launched your Token on a Bonding curve, and your best friend John wants to buy some. To make it easier, let's say that your Token is on a classic (linear) bonding curve and that the price of the first Token is $1. John will pay $1 for the first Token, $2 for the second, for the third, $3, and so on. To get the first ten tokens, John will have to pay $1+$2+$3+$4+....+$10, totaling at $55. Now, let's say your Mom wants to buy ten tokens. Your Mom's tokens price won't start at $1 but at $11 (as John already purchased the first ten tokens). Every new buyer pushed the price up by increasing the Supply. On the other hand, when someone sells a Token, it will be burnt (destroyed), will decrease the Supply, and will lower the Token price. If, for example, you bought the third token (at $3) ever created and decide to sell the same token a year later after 100 Tokens have been created. You'll sell your Token (originally bought at $3) at the price of the 100th token ($100) and decrease the Supply to 99. You'll make a profit of 100-3 = $97.

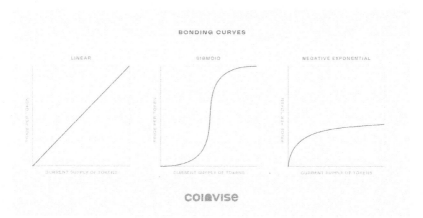

Three types of bonding curves: Linear, Sigmoid, and Negative Exponential Curve

There are many advantages to creating a token on a bonding curve. It guarantees Liquidity, allows a limitless Supply, reduces the volatility of the Token, and reduces the risks of hacks. However, it's more common to see communities minting their Token on a Fixed supply. Unless you're an expert and know what you're doing, we recommend creating a Token on a Fixed Supply. Indeed, it allows better usability, lowers entry barriers, gives community leaders full power over the distribution of the native Token, and doesn't require a strong community ready to pay from day one.

Now that you're aware of the two models, and considering you want to create a Token on a Fixed supply, you can start thinking of the total Supply you want to create. The standard is to create a supply of 10M, but again, some successful communities have thrived with less supply (e.g. Metafactory has a 420 000 total supply) or more (e.g. Bankless DAO has a 1 billion initial supply).

What's more important when considering creating a token is to think about the relative amount of tokens (i.e. what percentage of the total Supply are we talking about). For example, let's say you decide to create 100K tokens worth 100K dollars. It means that if someone buys 1000 tokens, he will have to pay $1000. If, in another scenario, you decide to create 1M tokens that are still worth 100K dollars, if someone pays $1000, he will get only 10K Tokens. In both cases, the person ending-up holding the same relative amount of tokens: 1% of all tokens. More than the total supply, while extremely important, you also have to think about the relative amount of token (i.e the percentage) when taking decision. Instead of thinking about the number of tokens you should put in the treasury, maybe it's better to think in percentages.

The price of the Token is also part of the Token Design and will be decided when community leaders will create a Liquidity pool (we'll get back to the concept of Liquidity Pool later in this chapter). The token's price and its volatility are vital components of Tokenomics. We'll talk further about it later in this chapter.

Token design is the first step in creating a Token, and it's not a small task. It's important to think about it thoroughly, depending on your use cases, as it will be complicated to increase the total supply if you realize it was not enough.

With the Token created and sent to a secured wallet, community leaders will have to think about distributing it to contributors.

2 - Token Distribution: How should a creator distribute the token to incentivize more people to help the project grow?

Once a creator has gathered a small and tight community (can be as few as ~20 people) and has created a Token, the second step is to think about how to reward these early believers. Thinking about how to incentivize them to continue building, and motivate some more people to join the community. It's always a big step when introducing a Token in a community, and it's essential to make it right.

The challenge with Token Distribution is to create efficient distribution mechanisms that would put the tokens in the hands of people willing to produce long-term work for the network. Your role, as a community leader, is to create a healthy community that can thrive in the long term, and the first step to accomplish this goal is to decide on what percentage of the supply should go in the treasury, to the stakeholders, as a retroactive airdrop etc..

There are several areas in your community where you can distribute your Token. You could choose for example to allocate a part of the supply to airdrop (send) tokens to members of other communities that are related to your project. Doing Airdrops can be an interesting way to attract potential contributors. You could also allocate part of the supply to the core team to motivate them build a great community or keep some tokens in the treasury to allocate them to community members that help the project grow. You have to think thoroughly about the percentage of the total supply you want to assign to the treasury. There is no rule of thumb for the treasury's percentage. Some communities have 15% of their supply allocated to their treasury, some 20%, and others 45%. The Treasury will help you fund exciting initiatives within the community.

There are two main ways to allocate Tokens to community members when creating a decentralized community: Bounties and budget allocations. There are fundamental differences between bounty hunters and core contributors, and it's essential to distribute the tokens accordingly.

Setting up bounties will serve for one-off missions. It can be extremely useful to attract more people to your community. Bounty hunters will usually participate very flexibly on an ad-hoc basis. They're ready to rent their time in exchange for Tokens but won't be involved in the vision and the day-to-day operations.

The second way to distribute tokens is to develop Guilds, or working groups, in charge of specific missions within the community. By creating these working groups, community leaders will allocate funds to specifics teams and organize the community more thoughtfully. Community members in those working groups are core contributors and Staff. They will take care of more complex missions, help run the day-to-day operations, and be committed in the long term.

In any case, bounty hunters and core contributors will be incentivized to work thanks to the Social Token, and having enough treasury to reward all the active community members is extremely important.

While the monetary value of the token can play a huge role in why people are contributing, the are many other rights and perks that can be assigned to token holders.

Indeed, once you've started distributing the token, you should reflect on the rights you want to give to token holders. In specific communities, owning a token bestows a right that results in product usage, a governance action, a given contribution, voting, or direct access to a product or market. For example, Global Coin Research's members holding the $GCR token have governance rights, can pool liquidity (stake), earn more tokens in doing so, have access to exclusive content, access to deals and events etc..

As the last piece of advice on token distribution, it's essential, specifically at the beginning, to consider any person to whom you give token an investor. With a very centralized community at the beginning (mostly the creator of the token or a small core team), each person that will receive the token will (potentially) have governance power and can have a huge influence over the future decisions of the community.

In most new communities, the only way to earn a token is to put some work in the community and be involved in it. Later on, however, community leaders should start opening the access to the community and allow anyone to buy tokens. This process is called "Pooling Liquidity" and comes with the concerns of price stability.

3 - Financial aspects: How creators can manage the stability of the token so people are still motivated to collaborate?

As in every project, the financial aspect is a critical component of a Social Token. A token that gains value (both social and financial value) will attract top talent and incentivize community members to become contributors.

First of all, it's important to explain briefly what gives value to a token.

At its creation, a Social Token created on a fixed supply has no inherent value, as no one has put money in it yet. You could have a million of a $NAME Token you've just created that you couldn't buy any item in real life. That's the reason why, at some point, communities are looking to add Liquidity, allowing anyone to buy the Token in exchange for some other cryptocurrencies that already have a monetary value. By allowing anyone to buy and sell the Token, the coin gains economic value, and community leaders can use this money to make the community grow.

Concretely, pooling liquidity means creating a Pool where people can make their Token and another one (bond) available for anyone wanting to buy it. When the Liquidity Pool is created, users can add the exact value of two Token (ex. $500 of your Token + $500 of collateral, aka any other token) in a Pool and earn trading fees proportional to their share of the total Liquidity. Put simply, these Liquidity providers facilitate trading by willing to buy or sell a particular asset at any given time, thereby providing Liquidity and enabling traders to trade without waiting for another buyer or seller to show up. The price is determined by Automated Market Maker directly on the Decentralized Exchange you're creating the pool on (ex: Uniswap). If you're still not sure to understand the concept of Liquidity Pool, don't worry, we'll dig into this throughout an entire chapter in the third part of this book.

With a better understanding of Social Token's financial value, it will be essential to understand how to manage the stability of the Token. Indeed, with a highly volatile token, contributors won't risk their time in exchange for a token that could plummet the day after. Likewise, a Token that can double in value overnight will attract only speculators, members that are only there for a quick buck and not keen to put some work to make the community grow and evolve.

There are many ways to limit the volatility of a token. The first one is to vest a portion of the supply. Concretely, vesting a token means locking a certain amount of tokens over a certain period as a commitment to hold the Token. When a token is vested, the owner of those Token can't withdraw them directly and have to wait until the vesting period ends. It's made possible thanks to blockchain mechanisms, and specifically smart contracts, that make it easy to lock a certain amount of funds until contract conditions are met. In our case, when the vesting period has been completed, the smart contract, enforced on a blockchain, will allow the holders to withdraw their tokens.

It is also possible to bond the Token with a stable coin in a Liquidity Pool to ensure price stability. Indeed, when creating a liquidity pool, while it's not the only factor that makes the price fluctuate, the Token with whom you're bonding your Token can have an impact on your token price. When bonding your Token with collateral volatile, if the price of this token drops considerably, it will, in a way, impact the price of your Token.

Thirdly, you can try to stabilize the price of the Token by creating Liquidity Mining Programs. Liquidity Mining is the same concept that having a savings account and making interests. When putting your money at the bank, you agree that bankers will play with your money in exchange for a specific interest rate. When pooling Liquidity on a decentralized exchange, you agree to automatically buy or sell a particular asset at any given time to help the project grow in exchange for a reward. It is a powerful way of incentivizing users to hold on to their crypto holdings, as, in return for doing so, these users will receive staking rewards. Creating Liquidity Mining Programs, and therefore having more Liquidity, will increase transaction depth. Transaction depth is the degree of market price stability. The greater the depth, the less significant the impact of several transactions will be on the price. On the other hand, with low Liquidity, a single person can drop or bump the cost of your Token by buying or selling a significant amount. Through

Liquidity Mining Programs, community leaders ensure to have enough Liquidity to grow their project and start a gradual path to community ownership. Liquidity Mining Programs have shown their efficiency to align incentives and create a positive-sum game.

As we've just seen, there are many financial tools at the disposal of community leaders to reduce the volatility of a token.

*

As seen in this chapter, all of the above elements will play a major role in the way people collaborate in a decentralized community. As a creator, it's important to think thoroughly about the Token design, Token Distribution, and Financial aspects of your Token to ensure the long-term success of the community. We've just seen multiple examples of concrete actions community leaders can take to incentivize a community to participate in the project, and that's what we call Tokenomics.

You will rapidly notice that thriving communities often have great Tokenomics. They have good mechanisms that make more people join the community and actively participate and create value.

While there is no one-size-fits-all solution to figure the Tokenomics of a project, this chapter should give you the basics and open your eyes on what's possible to do with a Token.

In the second part of this book, we've seen how to attract high-quality talents, design great incentives, crowdfund a project, and figure out the

Tokenomics of a project. We'll now dig more into the technical aspects of Social Tokens and explain other crucial concepts such as Liquidity Pool or Vesting Schedule.

III

Part Three: Technical aspects

In this part, we'll explore the technical aspects of Social Tokens. Several financial tools have shown their efficiency in making a community thrive, and we're going to explain in this part how they work and how you can leverage them.

10

Chapter 10: Layer 1 & Layer 2

Social tokens can be minted (created) on different blockchain. It is essential to understand that your tokens can exist on different blockchains. There different types of Blockchains: Layer 1 Blockchains and Layer 2 Blockchains. The two solutions have pros and cons, and the goal of this chapter is to help you navigate this to choose the best Blockchain depending on your needs.

As a friendly reminder, a blockchain is a digital ledger that stores all the transactions in a decentralized and secure way thanks to cryptographic mechanisms. Instead of relying on third parties such as banks to serve as the middleman in a transaction, you can securely send money without having to trust the recipient by doing it on a Blockchain. Every action taken on the Blockchain must be verified by others to be approved, making sure there is no fraud.

We'll go through what exactly is Layer 1 and Layer 2, and in which case you should use one or the other.

1 - What is Layer 1 & Layer 2 (L1&L2)?

L1 stands for Layer 1 (also called Ethereum Mainnet), which is the Ethereum Blockchain. It's the main network where every Transaction takes place. As mentioned above, transactions happening on the Ethereum Mainnet (L1) need to be verified by others to be approved. Users that verify the transactions are called *"Miners"* and to thank those contributors (*Miners*) for verifying a transaction and incentivizing them to make the network more secure, we give them a tip, a slice of the trade, also called *"Gas fees."*

Due to its infrastructure, the Ethereum Blockchain can currently process around 15 transactions per second. This infrastructure means that you'll sometimes have to wait hours before seeing your Transaction approved, while some users need their transactions to be approved quicker. Those users can offer more money to reward the *Miners* and see their transactions being approved in priority. As more and more people want to do transactions on the Blockchain and are keen to pay a higher price (*Gas fees*) to reward contributors (*Miners*), the price increases.

To solve this problem of paying high fees for every Transaction, projects have emerged to create another Blockchain on top of the Ethereum Blockchain. It's those blockchains that we're calling Layer 2. These other Blockchains (Layer 2) help increase Layer 1 by handling transactions off-chain and increasing the number of transactions that can happen simultaneously. These Layer 2 Blockchains use the exact Ethereum Blockchain mechanisms that make it easy for certain transactions to run through their network (Blockchain) while maintaining the same level of security. By creating copies of the original Ethereum blockchains, they offload transactions from the main chain and help reduce the gas fees (slice of the trade). Layer 2 is built on top of Layer 1 and doesn't replace nor be a competitor of the Ethereum Mainnet. Several Layer 2 blockchains exist, such as Polygon (Matic) Network, Optimism, or BSC, and these blockchains allow between 2k and 4k transactions per second (compared to 15/s on the Ethereum Blockchain).

2 - What are the implications for a Creator?

Now that you have a better understanding of the differences between Ethereum Mainnet (L1) or Polygon (Matic) Network (L2), you can make wiser decisions on which Blockchain to choose for certain transactions.

What is essential to understand is that this isn't necessarily binary, as your tokens can exist on different blockchains. Layer 1 might be preferable for High-Value Transactions (if you want to send a $5k worth NFT to the winner of an auction, for example). In contrast, Layer 2 might be more beneficial for High Volume Transactions (if you need to send a small number of your tokens to many people). We could compare Layer 1 with a Fedwire transfer and Layer 2 with an application like Venmo. You need both in your life, but the use cases are different. For small transactions such as sending $10 to some of your friends, it makes more sense to use Venmo (easier to make many small transfers, better mobile integration etc..). On the other hand, maybe it's more appropriate for high-value transactions to send a Fedwire transfer (If you need to pay your student loan, for example).

The rationale behind using Layer 2 instead of Layer 1 is the *Gas Fees*, as explained previously. The more transactions you're making, the more expensive the *Gas Fees* will be. If you're planning to airdrop (send) 1 token to 20 of your friends or community members, you'll have to run 20 transactions on the Blockchain, which can result in a lot of *Gas Fees* to pay. By running these "High Volume transactions" on the Polygon

(Matic) Network (L2), you'll save money. On the other hand, if you have to send a High-Value NFT, you'll have to run only one Transaction for a decent amount of money, which wouldn't make sense to make this Transaction on Layer 1.

Now, let's take a closer look at which Layer you should use for different use cases to make sure you've understood the difference between L1 & L2.

You should make the transactions on the Ethereum Mainnet (L1) for :

- *NFT drops* - If you need to send NFTs to a few people in your community (High-value transactions)
- *Pooling Liquidity* - If you need to create a Pool on Uniswap (one transaction of a possibly large number of tokens - High-Value Transaction)
- *Bounties* - You can set up bounties on Coinvise.co. If you need to outsource specific missions (Writing an article, do a design, make a video) and create bounties. It makes sense to use Layer 1 in this case, as you need only one person to complete the mission.

You should make the transactions on the Polygon (Matic) Network (L2) for :

- *Airdrop / Bulk transactions* - If you need to send tokens to many people (high-Volume transactions).
- *Rewards* - Comparable to airdrop. If you want to reward all (or a part) of your community (High-Volume Transaction), you should send the rewards through the Polygon (Matic) Network to save Gas fees.

*

At this point, you should understand better the dynamics behind making transactions on Layer 1 and Layer 2. Again, there is no right or wrong solution, and you should continuously adapt the number of tokens you have on each blockchain depending on your needs.

11

Chapter 11: Social Token as Financial Assets

As Social tokens grow in popularity, I often receive questions regarding the financial aspects of creating a Token. The two most common questions I hear are usually "what can you do with it?" and "Does my social Token have any value?"

What Social Tokens allow you, in the end, is unlocking different experiences with your community. You have control over the means and the production over what you create throughout the process. Instead of limiting the access (paywall in front of an article or a video), Web3 encourages collaboration and opens access to anyone wanting to build and collectively operate together. It's a complete paradigm shift.

There are two main ways to create a Token, as already seen in the Tokenomics chapter. The first one is to make your Token on a Fixed Supply Model ; you're creating a fixed supply of Token, the standard is 10M, and you can then distribute it to whoever you want in the way you want. The second one is to create it on a Bonding Curve Model ; you're creating your Token on a Bonding Curve, which means the supply starts at 0, and every new Token created will cost more than the previous one.

There is no right or wrong answer, but there are fundamental differences between creating on a Bonding curve and a Fixed supply, and it's essential to well understand those differences to make sure it fits your needs.

In this chapter, we'll go deeper on the financial aspect of creating a Token.

1 - The Fixed Supply Model

1.1 - What does that mean to create my Token on a Fixed Supply?

While we quickly talked about the different models to create a Token in the Tokenomics chapter, I feel like it's important to explore deeper those concepts.

The fixed supply model is a model where you define beforehand the number of tokens you want to create. Having a fixed supply allows you to get directly in your Crypto Wallet a known number of tokens that you can share or give to incentivize your community to participate in your project. The industry standard is to create 10 million of your tokens but you can define the number of tokens you want to create.

The fixed supply model works more around personal tokens. If you're a Creator that wants an easy solution to experiment with Social Token and create new experiences with your fan, you should hands down mint your token on a fixed supply.

The main advantages of creating your Social Token on a Fixed Supply model are:

- **Usability and lower barrier to entry** - Anyone can create its Token on a Fixed Supply. You'll receive the tokens in your Crypto Wallet and can then distribute them the way you want. You don't technically need a pre-existing community willing to buy your first Token. They are already created and exist on the blockchain.
- **Full power over the distribution of the native Token** - Centralized control over your token Supply prevents anyone from buying a significant amount of your token and using them in a harmful way. A safe and sustainable distribution strategy is critical for some projects - you must get your Token into the right people's hands if you want the project to succeed. With the Fixed Supply model, you have the full power over the distribution.

However, in creating your Token on a Fixed Supply, you'll be limited at one point if your project grows exponentially as you won't be able to increase the supply. It's also good to remember that when building on a Fixed supply, your Token has no inherent value as you're the owner of most of the supply, and no one has put money into your project. With a token based on a fixed supply, you'll create experiences that don't require inherent value. Experiences that only live in your economy. We could think of a "control my life" type of experience, gated articles or content (your fans will need enough of your Token to read the article), tips for spontaneous help, etc.

Creating a token allows you to better collaborate with your community and create a new kind of relationship with your fans. Again, you own all the supplies, which means that the experience you're creating only lives in your economy (we can't redeem anything IRL for your Token) and that owning your Token is a social asset, collectible value, that your fans will be proud to own. Maybe more a "nice-to-have" than "must-have".

As we've just seen, there are pros and cons to creating a Social Token on a Fixed Supply.

It's also good to mention that creating your Token on a fixed supply doesn't mean it will never have monetary value, and you can create a Liquidity Pool, set an initial price, and allow anyone to buy your Token. By doing so, you'll allow anyone to buy your Token and, therefore, opening the doors for more people to join your economy and participate in your projects.

Adding value to your Token is not the first thing you should do when creating one. Indeed, you should first focus on making actual use cases for your Token and gather a strong community around your project. Without a strong community, you won't increase your Token's value as no one will be keen to buy it. Creating a liquidity pool is more a later stage action when you'll want to accomplish new (and maybe more significant) projects than part of the initial tasks you should make when creating a token.

Let's get into the fun part of Social Tokens: The liquidity Pools (LP).

2 - Liquidity Pool

2.1 - What is a liquidity Pool (LP)?

Put simply, creating a Liquidity pool means providing Liquidity for potential buyers. When you're creating a social Token, this Token has no inherent value. You could have one million of your $NAME Token, it wouldn't make you a millionaire in our society. Creating a liquidity pool (LP) allows anyone to buy your Token in exchange for other cryptocurrencies with value in USD. When the LP is created, a liquidity provider sets both assets' initial price and equal supply. A liquidity pool is a collection of funds locked in a smart contract. Users can add the exact value of two Token (your Token + collateral, aka any other token) in a Pool and earn trading fees proportional to their share of the total Liquidity.

Liquidity Pools are most commonly set up on Uniswap, a trustless, decentralized exchange for Ethereum. If you're unfamiliar with Uniswap, it's a DeFi (Decentralized Finance) protocol that lets anyone add Liquidity (ETH + an equivalent dollar value of a token) to a pool (a collection of Liquidity from anyone, anywhere in the world.)

Users putting Liquidity in a pool are named Liquidity Providers, and they make a % of fees on every trade in the pools they participate in and are therefore incentivized to add Liquidity. Put simply, these Liquidity providers facilitate trading by willing to buy or sell a particular asset at any given time, thereby providing Liquidity and enabling traders to trade without waiting for another buyer or seller to show up.

Indeed, in many markets, there may not be enough organic Liquidity to support active trade. This means that, as your Token is new, the chances are low that every time someone wants to buy one, there will be someone ready to sell it at a fair price. So when you're executing a trade on Uniswap, you don't have a counterparty in the traditional sense. There doesn't need to be a seller for the buyer to buy at that moment, thanks to the Liquidity providers who have already put some of your Token in a Pool, waiting for anyone to buy it.

Concretely, if you have some ETH you would like to swap (exchange) with the Creator's Token, you would go in the $ETH/$NAME pool and make the transaction there. The number of Liquidity Pools you can create for your Token is mostly infinite. If you create pools with your Token and many other collaterals (Other crypto tokens), your fans will have the choice to buy your Token with a lot of other cryptocurrencies. Such as you can go to your bank and ask to exchange your EUR in USD because the bank has some liquidity in dollars (money in a safe deposit box that the bank can give you directly), you want your community members to be able to go on Uniswap and exchange their cryptocurrencies in your $NAME Token.

2.2 - So why would you need to pool Liquidity for your Token?

You will need to pool Liquidity if you want to create a project that requires collaboration. By pooling liquidity, you'll drive the value of your Token, define its price and allow anyone to purchase it.

While centralized exchanges match buyers and sellers to determine prices and execute trades, taking a fee on the transaction, Uniswap uses a simple math equation and pools of tokens and ETH to do the same job. By knowing the balance between the ETH and your $NAME token in a pool (supply & demand), the equation can determine the price of a particular token whenever someone buys your $NAME Token with ETH. If your $NAME Token supply decreases while the supply of ETH increases, your $NAME token price goes up.

Also, by creating a Liquidity Pool, you'll create a place where anyone can buy your token and therefore participate in the project you're building. By letting your community members invest in your project early, they will give you an equivalent dollar value of a token (ETH or BTC, for example) in exchange for some of your $NAME Tokens. It will give ownership to your fans and, as the value of your token increases (considering more people are buying it and assuming you still own a decent amount of your Token), you'll get more money to realize your project.

Building on a Fixed Supply and creating on a later stage Liquidity Pools is a great strategy for personal Token (if you're a solo creator) as you can in first time gather a strong community around a joint project, then, in a second time, crowdfund your project, bootstrap liquidity and ask your community members to supply Liquidity to facilitate trade on Uniswap.

However, suppose you're creating a community around a broad vision (e.g., BanklessDAO) or building a protocol (e.g., Rarible protocol or Zora). In that case, it might be preferable to create your Token on a Bonding curve.

3 - The Bonding Curve Model

3.1 - What does that mean to create a token on a bonding curve?

The core idea of minting a token on a bonding curve is that its price increases as the supply or distribution of the Token does. The more tokens have been distributed, the higher the price. This means that early adopters can buy the Token at a much cheaper rate than when the supply increases over time.

Let's take an example to illustrate what a bonding curve is. You've just launched your Token on a Bonding curve, and your best friend John wants to buy some. To make it easier, let's say that your Token is on a classic (linear) bonding curve and that the price of the first Token is $1. John will pay $1 for the first Token, $2 for the second, for the third, $3, and so on. This means for John to get the first ten tokens, he will have to pay $1+$2+$3+$4+$5. Totaling at $55.

Now, let's say your Mom wants to buy ten tokens. Your Mom's tokens price won't start at $1 but at $11 (as John already purchased the first ten tokens). Every new buyer pushed the price up by increasing the supply.

On the other hand, when someone sells a Token, it will be burnt (destroyed), decrease the supply, and lower the Token price. People that have bought your Token early (at a low price) and have believed early in your project will be rewarded by being able to resell their Token at a Higher price as the price is increasing with the supply (the more people believing in your project, the more the price of your Token will increase).

Creating your Token on a bonding curve greatly facilitates giving value to the token and allowing you to determine how the discovery price will work in the future. Indeed, a bonding curve has its own AMM (Automated Market Maker – a mathematical function that defines the price of your Token depending on different parameters) that allows you to choose the best model of bonding curve depending on your needs. You have way more freedom over the price discovery of your Token with a token minted on a bonding curve than on a fixed supply, and you can choose the type of bonding curve you want, depending on your needs.

2.2 - Which type of bonding curve?

Before minting your Token, you have to choose which type of bonding curve you want. There are different use cases depending on the bonding curve you select. We won't go too deep into the different types of bonding curves, but you should have a good overview of what's possible and the use cases for each model, thanks to the graphic below.

The Reserve Ratio determines how sharply a Continuous Token's price needs to adjust to being maintained with every transaction. The Reserve Ratio determines the price sensitivity of a Token and, by playing with it, you can create different models of bonding curves. We will cover three types of bonding curves: Linear, Sigmoid, and Negative Exponential Curve.

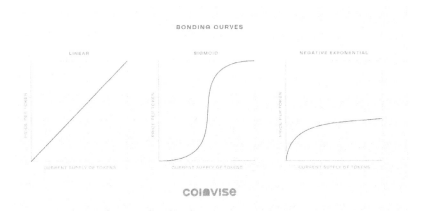

Linear bonding curve: A Linear "Classic" bonding curve allows a fixed and predetermined price discovery mechanism that rewards people for investing in you early.

Sigmoid bonding Curve: A Sigmoid Bonding curve is recommended for projects that reward the first believers (early investors) and set a high price for the late joiner. This bonding curve suits Meme, for example, where the first believers, those who hype up the project since the beginning, will profit over the people who join the project once it's already mainstream. People who have joined before the inflection point will earn profit while others will likely lose money as the price will increase sharply after the inflection point.

Negative Exponential Curve: This curve is recommended for projects such as crowdfunding, when you want to reward the first believers but don't want the late joiners to pay a high price as no one would help anymore past a cap.

As we've just seen, minting (creating) your Token on a Bonding Curve gives you more freedom over its price discoverability, and you should take the time to think about your use-cases to choose the best solution.

Now that we've covered what a Fixed supply model, a liquidity pool, and a Bonding curve are, you should clearly understand the differences between them. As mentioned before, the fixed supply model and the bonding curve model are entirely different and are not made for the same use cases.

To make it easier to understand, we'll make a quick recap here covering the main differences between the fixed Supply and the bonding curve models and the pros and cons of each model.

Main advantages of creating your Social Token on a Fixed Supply model

:

- **Usability and lower barrier to entry** - Anyone can create its Token on a Fixed Supply. You'll receive the tokens in your Crypto Wallet and can then distribute them the way you want. You don't technically need a pre-existing community willing to buy your first tokens. They are already created and exist on the blockchain. You own the whole Supply from day 1.
- **Full power over the distribution of the native Token** - Centralized control over your token Supply prevents anyone from buying a significant amount of your token and using them in a harmful way. A safe and sustainable distribution strategy is critical for some projects - you must get your Token into the right people's hands if you want the project to succeed.
- **Easier if you're a solo creator creating a personal token** - The Fixed Supply model will allow you to take your time and think thoroughly about the way you want to build your project. By owning the whole Supply, you can allocate your tokens the way you want.
- **You don't need a strong community that is ready to pay from day one** - As you own the total Supply, you can take your time to gather a strong community around a joint project. This is a great advantage compared to the Bonding curve model as, in the bonding curve model, the early adopters might buy the Token. Still, if the community is not big and strong enough, as the price rises, no one will buy tokens anymore and can kill the project.

Main advantages of creating your Social Token on a Bonding Curve model :

- **Guaranteed Liquidity** - you can create a contract and have anyone be able to buy and sell your token right away. It can help bootstrap awareness and interest as backers know they have Liquidity from day one. Tokens can be purchased or sold instantaneously as the bonding curve act as an automated market maker (Market makers are agents that alleviate this problem by facilitating trade that would otherwise not occur. "Automated market makers" (AMMs) are algorithmic agents that perform those functions and, as a result, provide Liquidity in electronic markets. AMM buys some of your tokens and agrees to sell them at any given time to anyone wanting to buy your Token.)

- **Reduced volatility** - in times of changing demand for the Token, the bonding curve allows *both the price and Supply* to adjust in response. Deterministic price calculation decreases the size and probability of boom and bust cycles that frequently plague fixed-supply tokens. Also, it ensures a continuous price. The price of your Token will always be $n-1<n<n+1$.

- **Limitless Supply** - There is no limit to the number of tokens that can be minted. You have no limits on how big your project can become.

- **You have complete power over the future discovery price of your Token** - As seen in this chapter, you can adapt it depending on your needs.

- **Reduces the risks of hacks** - If your platform or project is hacked, as you don't own all the Supply, it limits the risks. Tokens belong to the users that bought them and are on their wallets.

- **Easier for a protocol or a community with more options** - You usually don't know the Supply you need as you don't know if your project will grow exponentially. With a bonding curve, as long as there is demand, it will be possible to create new tokens.

*

To conclude this chapter, If you want an easy solution for your personal Token, you should go with a fixed supply model for your Token. On the other hand, if you're a big community founder or the Creator of a protocol that wants to launch a token, maybe you should consider creating a bonding curve and exploring the pros and cons of the different types of bonding curves.

12

Chapter 12: Liquidity Mining (staking) for social tokens

While communities can have different needs depending on their goals, vision, and missions, almost every community at a particular stage need to incentivize its contributor to pool Liquidity. Indeed, having Liquidity for a community is crucial, and community leaders, at some point, will have to find a way to aligned interests and convinced contributors to make available a part of their Token to anyone wanting to buy it.

So how can community leaders incentivize contributors to provide Liquidity?

The answer is: by allowing Liquidity Mining. With Liquidity Mining programs, contributors will earn money by pooling liquidity. Thanks to the Liquidity now available, the community will grow and work on more significant projects.

Liquidity Mining Programs (LMP) are a fantastic tool to leverage a community. This chapter aims to explain to a broader audience that might not be familiar with those concepts what Liquidity Mining programs are and how, as someone new in the Social Token space, you can help a community to grow while earning social tokens. Let's get into it.

1 - What is Liquidity?

Today, many of the most famous decentralized communities have created a Token on a Fixed supply, which means they have made a known number of tokens since day one, and then reflected on how to allocate and distribute them.

As we just saw in the previous chapter creating a Liquidity Pool means allowing anyone to buy and sell the Token. The Token will then gains economic value, and community leaders will use this money to make the community grow. Pooling liquidity is a good way for communities to leverage their early believers to crowdfund their projects and build a treasury for future needs.

At the very beginning, the main goal of a community leader is to gather a strong community toward a joint project and reward manually contributors that are early believers in the project. Community leaders have total power over the token distribution and can control each action taken for the community. However, at a later stage, a community should decentralize the power and open its economy to more people interested in joining, allowing anyone to buy/sell the community Token. By purchasing Tokens, buyers will become contributors and have voting power over future decisions, making the community more decentralized.

To summarize, in the first phase of a community, the only way to earn some of the Social Tokens is to contribute and be rewarded manually by community leaders who have access to the whole supply. However, in a later stage, community leaders should create a Liquidity pool and make available the community token in exchange for USD or other cryptocurrencies with monetary value to decentralize more the community and crowdfund future needs.

As we just saw, most communities need Liquidity at some point. But how do you find this Liquidity? How do you incentivize the early contributors of your community, those who earned a decent amount of Tokens, to provide Liquidity for the community? How do you convince them to deposit the Token on a decentralized exchange to provide Liquidity for the community?

A solution that has shown its efficiency in the past is the Liquidity Mining Programs, and we're going to dig into this right now.

2 - Liquidity Mining Programs

Liquidity mining, also known as yield farming, provides Liquidity via cryptocurrencies to decentralized exchanges. It's the process of depositing or lending specified token assets to Provide Liquidity to the community's fund pool and obtain an income afterward.

Liquidity Mining is the same concept that having a savings account and making interests. When putting your money at the bank, you agree that bankers will play with your money in exchange for a specific interest rate. When pooling Liquidity on a decentralized exchange, you agree to automatically buy or sell a particular asset at any given time to help the project grow in exchange for a reward. It is a powerful way of incentivizing users to hold on to their crypto holdings, as, in return for doing so, these users will receive staking rewards.

To make it more clear, here are the conditions of the Liquidity Mining Program created by Forefront, a thriving community with the goal of creating exclusive content and market insights on Social Tokens and DAOs:

"Forefront will allocate 20,000 FF from the treasury for this program that will get distributed to FF/ETH Uniswap V2 liquidity providers over 60 days. The reward will be distributed proportionally to the amount of Liquidity each person provides. i.e. if you provide $4,000 worth of Liquidity ($2,000 FF & $2,000 ETH) and there is a total of $100k Liquidity in the FF-ETH pool for ten days, then you are entitled to 10% of the distribution over that period."

Pooling Liquidity is expensive. As you have to bond your Token with another one that has monetary value, if you want to put $100K worth of your Token in a pool, you'll also have to deposit $100K worth of another token. By creating such a program and allocating a part of their treasury to reward contributors that would participate, Forefront's Leaders ensured to motivate enough people to pool Liquidity and leveraged the power of its community.

While the monetary aspect is central in Liquidity Mining Programs and is often the main reason people agree to hold their token and pool Liquidity, there are many other advantages of creating and participating in such programs for contributors and Community leaders.

3 - Use cases

For a community, Liquidity is essential. Indeed, with enough Liquidity, communities will:

- **Start a gradual path to community ownership** - By allowing anyone to buy and sell the Token, more people will have the Token and have the voting power that comes with it. Liquidity is an excellent way to decentralize the decision power and a path to community Ownership. are now official community owners and govern the Braintrust network. You're able to use your tokens to vote on key decisions and to control the future of the platform you make your living on.

- **Be able to bootstrap the project** - With people exchanging other cryptocurrencies that have monetary value for the $NAME Token, community leaders have access to funds that they can use to fund new experiences and grow the community.

- **Increase the transaction speed** - If Liquidity is low, there's a high probability that your orders will take a lot of time to be executed. On the other hand, with a lot of Liquidity, the processing of orders takes only a few seconds.

- **Transaction depth** - Transaction depth is the degree of market price stability. The greater the depth, the less significant the impact of several transactions will be on the price. On the other hand, with low Liquidity, a single person can drop or bump the cost of your Token by buying or selling a significant amount.

Creating Liquidity pools and Liquidity Mining programs are important milestones for every community as it comes with many advantages. But it's also highly interesting for contributors as it gives them more ownership over the project (Pool liquidity > earn tokens as a reward > more tokens = more voting power) and allow a broader and equal distribution of the Token. Liquidity Mining Programs lower barriers to entry and give any individual an equal chance of owning tokens. Contributors don't need to be accredited investors or have tons of money to invest in projects they like. They can earn a decent amount of Social Token by pooling Liquidity and claim the rewards.

*

Liquidity Mining is an excellent way for anyone to invest in promising communities and earn Social Tokens. Through Liquidity Mining Programs, community leaders ensure to have enough Liquidity to grow their project and start a gradual path to community ownership. Liquidity Mining Programs have shown their efficiency to align incentives and create a positive-sum game.

13

Chapter 13: What is Vesting Schedule?

With Social Tokens comes the risk of speculation. Speculation is not necessarily a bad thing. It drives interest from people outside of crypto and
brings capital to a community that can innovate and grow. It is, however,
very complicated to build a healthy and sustainable community in the
long-term with a highly volatile token and community members here
to speculate. At some point, for a community to grow, it's essential
to have people that put time and hard work into the community, not
capital.

To prevent speculation, community leaders can lock N amount of Token
for a certain period as a commitment to hold the Token. It prevents
people from coming with the only purpose of buying and selling the
Token a few days later when it pumps. This mechanism is called Vesting
Schedule. This chapter aims to explain further what a Vesting Schedule
is and how it can be a powerful tool to build a sustainable decentralized
community.

1 - What is Token Vesting?

When launching a decentralized community (or a DAO), it's common to establish a Token for governance purposes and for attracting / rewarding high-quality talent. The Token is usually minted (created) by the community's founding members, and those community leaders have full power over the distribution of the Token.

This is much power centralized in the hands of very few people. If contributors start to put time into the project and investors start to bring capital to the project, it's important to cover them and not let core team members have full freedom over the token distribution. To prevent bad behaviors, it's recommended to vest a portion of those tokens to ensure the long time commitment of the founding team.

Concretely, vesting a token means locking a certain amount of tokens over a certain period as a commitment to hold the Token. It's a mechanism that allows the founding team to prove they are highly interested in the project.

Locking tokens ensures investors that the team has the best intention and maintains a long-term vision, incentivizing them to continue working on the project development. When a token is vested, the owner of those Token can't withdraw them directly and have to wait until the vesting period ends. It's made possible thanks to blockchain mechanisms, and specifically smart contracts, that make it easy to lock a certain amount of funds until contract conditions are met. In our case, when the vesting period has been completed, the smart contract, enforced on a blockchain, will allow the holders to withdraw their tokens.

Depending on the needs, it's possible to play on many parameters when vesting a Token. It's possible to play with the vesting period, the number of tokens subject to vesting, if the tokens will be released gradually etc... It's important to keep in mind that there is no right or wrong answer. A project could reserve 15% of its coins when the Token is minted, then gradually released some tokens every month/quarter/year during the project process. Another project could create a Community Round subject to vesting, with a vesting period that includes a 6-month cliff, followed by another six-month linear unlock. In this case, community members would receive a certain amount of Token, let's say 1200, but wouldn't be able to withdraw them for six months. They would then receive 200 tokens every month for six months.

Keeping a certain amount of Token on a vesting schedule is a powerful tool to incentivize people to invest in a community. Crypto mechanisms made it easy for community members, investors, and founders to trust each other. With smart contracts, vesting a token is easy and is a tool worth using for every community. Let's dig more into the main advantages of the Vesting Schedule.

2 - What is it useful for?

To create a healthy and sustainable community, it is essential to have token price stability. Indeed, with a highly volatile token, it will be difficult to attract talent keen to work in exchange for a Token that can plummet overnight. Vesting a Token allows reducing the price volatility of a token by disincentivizing speculation. Indeed, suppose speculators know they won't be able to withdraw their money as soon as they want. In that case, eventually, they won't invest. Only true believers of the project will stay around. Vesting a token ensures the investors that the founding team is serious encourages contributors to commit in the long-term and prevents speculation.

The vesting schedule mechanism is particularly useful:

- **For treasury diversification** - when allowing community members to claim a token in exchange for some other tokens such as Ethereum, it can be useful to vest the tokens to ensure the long-term commitment of the new investors. It will limit the volatility of the Token for a certain period. It creates a fair process that rewards purchasers who support the project at launch and do so throughout the project's lifecycle by holding or utilizing the Token.
- **For crowdfunding** - Instead of receiving a total share of their tokens after the crowdfunding, the team members receive tokens after regularly scheduled vesting periods determined by the project founders. This way, alone unscrupulous team members can't run off with tokens without contributing to the project.

Let's also dig more into the main advantages of vesting a token.

- **Vesting shows that the team is highly interested in the project** - Locking tokens ensure investors that the team has the best intention and maintain a long-term vision for the project, incentivize them to continue working on the project development.
- **Vesting lowers market price manipulations** - There is often a several-year "cliff," meaning that the individual must be with the company for a couple of years to release the first increment of tokens.
- **Vesting limits the risk that few entities control a large proportion of the project's tokens** - It prevents the small group of people present when the supply has been minted to create supply fluctuations that can be ultimately damaging to the Token's ecosystem

and price.

· **Vesting helps keep the power centralized until the community is strong enough to be decentralized** - When rewarding a community through Tokens, it's better if the core team managed the token supply and transactions and kept the voting power centralized. By doing so, they'll have a firmer grasp of the token prices and will be able to build a strong and sustainable community.

It's also good to keep in mind that the more the already distributed tokens are used, the more valuable the reserved ones become, so it's in each project team member's best interest to create a successful project that has many users, increasing the value of their tokens in the process.

*

Having a token over a vesting schedule is an efficient way to protect investors, founders, and collaborators. Indeed, as shown in this chapter, locking a certain amount of Token allows to disincentivize founders and early investors to sell all their tokens with early traction. It also disincentivizes contributors to come only for speculation purposes.

14

Chapter 14: Social Token's Legal Aspects

Before minting your Token, there are general rules that you should be aware of if you don't want to have problems regarding the Law. First of all, it's essential to know that the SEC is in charge of regulating decentralized projects. The Securities and Exchange Commission (SEC) is a U.S. government oversight agency responsible for regulating the securities markets and protecting investors. It has a three-part mission: Protect investors. Maintain fair, orderly, and efficient markets. Facilitate capital formation.

The current regulation suggests Tokens should have as a main utility to offer fans new experiences within digital economies, which means they should buy Token in hopes of special perks instead of getting financial rewards. Indeed, a token that delivers promises or implies the possibility of any financial return is much more likely to be a security. For example, a use case that can have problems with the Law could be a Social Token as an ISA (Income Share Agreement). Offering a slice of your future revenue to token holders can be seen as a security, even though it's one of the most exciting use cases. If you want to create a token to share your future earnings with your community, you should be very cautious and ask a lawyer before doing it.

The Supreme Court is saying about Crypto that if a project is raising money selling a token and the buyers are anticipating profit, chances are it will be considered a Security.

Tokens should rather have as a primary utility to incentive communities thanks to non-economic advantages. For example, we could think of Social Advantages, where token holders genuinely do not expect to profit from the tokens and hold them for other reasons such as free access to members-only content, 1:1 call etc.. Even without economic value, your Token can have many social values and unlock new experiences that live in your own economy. A useful token, which means a Token without the sole interest of earning money, is less likely to be a security.

Of course, if a Token has a monetary value, it will be tricky to do so. The Law suggests to any community leader to clarify that financial value is not the primary purpose of a Token and that token holders have access to benefits accessible only for them.

Keeping the total power over the Token distribution with a token minted on a fixed supply will be easier. If a Token is transferable (for example, if it's minted on a Bonding curve or if the Token has Liquidity Pools), the Token's creator won't be able to limit the speculations.

The Supreme Court also warn token creators to be careful with False Advertising Issues. If the Token allows fans to access premium experiences, it's obliged that those benefits are really as "exclusive" as advertised.

Again, the fewer financial rewards involved in your project, the better.

Here are some incentives that can be considered as security:

- Don't allow your token holders to earn a return for holding your Token.
- Don't promise to pay (directly or indirectly) token holders (for work they could do, for example).
- Don't allow "Yield farming" or A 'buy-and-burn' models (redirect the revenues or profits to increase the value of the Token).

It's also good to remember that it's essential to have Clear Disclosure of Terms like any other reward or loyalty program. People buying Tokens should clearly understand what they're buying and how they earn and receive rewards.

*

There is still quite a bit of a grey area around the legal aspects of Social Token. Still, in general, if the sole use of your Token is to raise money and advertise to buyers that they will earn profits, chances are it will be considered a Security by the Supreme Court.

In the first three parts of this book, you respectively learned what DAOs and Social Tokens are, the new tools at your disposal to grow a tokenized community (incentives, crowdfunding...) and the technical aspects of Crypto such as Layer 1 & Layer 2, Vesting Schedule and Liquidity Mining Programs.

In the last part of this book, we will explore the future of this space and what new things can be built using these new decentralized tools.

IV

Part Four: The Future of Web3 and Social Tokens

In the last part of this book, we'll explore what the future of Web3 could look like and deep-dive into new concepts such as reputation score and interoperability.

15

Chapter 15: How to build a Decentralized Social Network?

In a recent essay, "Crypto-Bezos", Packy McCormick explains how Jeff Bezos, founder of Amazon, realized that whatever he would build needed to be something that could only exist online on the Internet.

Back in 1999, in an interview video, Bezos explained that "if you can do things using the more traditional method, you probably should do them using the more traditional method." Back in these days, Jeff Bezos already knew that he needed to leverage the Internet. He knew Amazon could only exist because of the Internet.

But being on the Internet wasn't the value proposition of Amazon. Nor being on the Web3 will be the value proposition of the next billion dollars companies. What's so exciting with Web3 is that it has the power to create completely new experiences and use-cases that have never been seen before. Comparable to what Jeff Bezos, founder of Amazon, did 20 years ago by completely reinventing the way people were buying books, we'll see Web3 companies reinvent things that we're doing today and 10x improve the experience.

So what are some of the experiences that can be reinvented in Web3? What are the areas that really need to leverage this new technology to 10x the experience?

Social Networks might be a good place to start. Indeed, for the last year, we've seen the creator economy booming, and we see more talented individuals sharing content online and gathering knit communities. More individuals are collaborating toward joint projects. Last year has proved to us that generation Z now wants to live from their passion and is not ready to follow the work paradigm that has been shaped during the last 50 years. The future of work is being built now. And most of the collaboration happens through current Social Networks (Discord, Twitter, Slack et..). But with our society evolving, these social networks don't fulfill our needs anymore. Creators today need Ownership and efficient ways to collaborate.

Web2 social platforms won't solve these problems because they intrin-sically can't. Resolving these would mean killing their business.

And that's when Web3 is coming. Decentralized Social networks have the power to solve these problems. Let me explain.

1 - The problems with Web2 Social Networks

From 00' to 10', we saw social networking and User Generated Content platforms rise. We saw the emergence of social media, which allowed everyone to have a voice on the Internet and express their creativity through their content. During the next decade, some users amassed millions of followers and started to monetize their content. Creators, also called 'Influencers' at this time, discovered they could monetize their audience through those platforms and that it was possible to earn a living from their passion. They were helping others (brands & businesses) to achieve their goals.

But the Internet and our society have evolved. After 10 years of working for brands, creators discovered they could now BE the brand, BE the product, and they could do for them what they were doing for others. Creators have new needs that current social media won't be able to solve.

Indeed, there are three main problems with current social media: Lock-in data, Centralized Power, and an Ads-driven Business model.

- **Lock-in Data** - Our physical and digital lives are intrinsically linked, and online Reputation is more important than ever. However, for 99% of people on the Internet, the value of their digital identity is locked within platforms. Creators that have built an audience of 1 million followers on Instagram won't start in another platform like Twitter with 1 million followers. They will begin with 0. Amazon sellers who have built their Reputation for years won't start on other marketplaces with five-star reviews. They will begin at 0. When leaving a platform, users have to start from scratch, all over again, as there is no interoperability between platforms. The data are locked. It doesn't incentivize users to do their best or build long-term relationships as they know they will lose it when leaving the platform. Furthermore, we cannot keep locating our social connections and memories inside servers controlled by for-profit companies. The connections between people should be controlled by the people, not by companies. Decentralized Social networks must re-capture our social data in new ways.
- **Centralized Power** - Today, social media is hyper-centralized. A handful of private companies control public discourse and earn profits off content they don't even create.

· **Ads-driven business model -** This outdated business model forces current social networks to keep a walled garden around their content. Indeed, opening their data would mean killing their business model. Their main way to monetize is to sell those data to for-profit companies to target specific audiences. This business model prevents external developers from innovating or building apps on top of it. It also gives users and creators no choice but to continue using these apps as they have already created an audience on these platforms. On top of that, this business model creates a situation where creators who actually produce the content are underpaid, under-monetized, and don't fully capture the value they are making.

We're now entering the third phase of Social media. Today's Creators don't want to do the promotion of products to their audience. They realized they could build big projects with their fans, involving them in the process and sharing the upsides with them. It's a complete paradigm shift in the fan/creator relationship. Today, Social Networks can't provide the tools needed to develop this kind of relationship.

So, what are precisely the needs of those creators? How can we build decentralized Social Networks that really empower them? What can of use-cases would appear on those platforms?

The first step to answering these questions is learning from the past and seeing what social mechanisms worked in Web2 platforms.

2 - Social mechanisms of current Social Network

Before exploring the possible use-cases of decentralized Social Networks, it's essential to understand what makes a good Social Network. By analyzing the dynamics of the current Social Networks, we'll understand more the Human Social Mechanisms and better understand how to leverage crypto mechanisms to fulfill these human needs.

2.1 - Proof of X

Julian Lehr developed the proof-of-X mechanism in his famous "Proof of X" essay. In this essay, he argues that, at their core, social networks are primarily about one thing: Building social capital through signaling. People are going on Instagram to prove they are creative (Proof-of-creative-work), on Wikipedia to prove they are knowledgable (Proof-of-knowledge), and on Strava to prove they are athletic (Proof-of-Physical-activity). As Julian mentioned in his essay (talking about Strava), "*While the status game that initially got you into the app might be zero-sum, the actual physical exercise you have to put in to compete has a very positive, compounding effect.*"

Creating a Social Network with a strong positive feedback loop will make sure people will come on the platform because it is actually good for them. They will come back repeatedly because it makes them feel good and because it's actually good for them. And the more you use the app, the more likely you are to do the atomic behavior. That's what a positive-sum game is all about. No one needs to lose for someone else to win. We can create Decentralized Social Networks that are viable and actually good for people.

The question is: What kind of social networks could have similar positive feedback loops? An exciting model explored is the play-to-earn model, where users have to do specific tasks to get rewarded.

For example, we could think of a Social Network that incentivizes its users to set up challenges and inspire others to do "sustainable life hacks (e.g. eat one vegan meal a day). Users could document it via short-form video and getting points related to their in-app activity: the number of actions/challenges completed, how many users they inspired to do the challenge etc.. Impactr is a community that is already exploring these mechanisms.

2.2 - Status-as-a-Service

In his famous essay "Status-as-a-Service," Eugene Wei argues that *"People are status-seeking monkeys"* and *"People seek out the most efficient path to maximizing social capital."*

To create a successful social network, it's essential to consider its utility and the Social Capital it can provide to users. Can I use the social network to accumulate social capital? How is it measured? And how do I earn that status? What kind of features can be implemented to reinforce this Social Status?

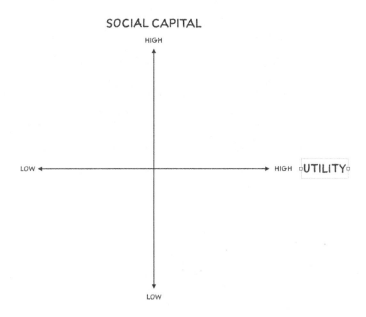

Users are going on Snapchat to discuss with friends, but then keep talking to not lose their "streaks" (number of consecutive days you're talking to someone). People are going on Twitter to post their journey but then try to get the "official" stamp.

It's crucial to understand that status must be earned the hard way. Otherwise, it wouldn't be worth anything. Value is tied to scarcity, and scarcity on social networks derives from proof-of-X. As explained right before, the proof-of-physical activity on Strava rewards users who are achieving impressive training sessions. The longer the bike ride you're doing, the more social capital you're gaining. Status isn't worth much if there's no skill and effort required to have it.

2.3 - Social Asymptote

Social Asymptote is a term I first heard in the "Status Monkey" essay by Packy McCormick. He explains that not everyone can do what it takes to gain social capital on any given social network, which creates an upper limit. There are only so many people you can convince to do the atomic behavior. Indeed, a lot of people nowadays have a TikTok account, but only a few of them are actually making videos on the platform. This is explained by the fact that it's not that easy to get familiar with all the tools the app allows. Most users are unwilling to put in the work to get good at whatever the TikTok algorithm requires. While it's impossible to have all the users of a platform actually publishing content and doing the atomic behavior, it's interesting to think about the mechanisms that can be put in place to encourage anyone to do it.

2.4 - Come for the tools, stay for the network.

In his famous essay "Come for the tool, stay for the network," Chris Dixon explains his idea to initially attract users with a single-player tool and then, over time, get them to participate in a network. The tool helps get to the initial critical mass. The network creates long-term value for users and defensibility for the company.

For example, Strava is attracting users by letting them track their sport activity easily (tool) and then publish the activity automatically in the profile of the users where other users can see, like, and comment on it (network).

Through these four examples we've just seen in the first part of this chapter, we know understand that to create a successful Decentralized

Social Network, we need to create a platform that effectively:

- Let users earn status the hard way.
- Makes users come back repeatedly because it makes them feel good and because it's actually good for them.
- Allows its users to do the atomic behaviors easily, and that actually encourages anyone to do it.
- Provides tools that make the life of the users more effortless, and therefore hook them.
- Solves the existing problems in Social Networks of Lock-in data, Centralized Power, and Ads-driven Business model.

3 - How to build a decentralized social network?

The best Social Networks have succeeded in reinventing the way people communicate together, reinventing the medium, and effectively leveraging human psychological behaviors. People first got hooked in those socials because it was new and allowed complete new behaviors. I think Web3 platforms will hook the next billions of social media users by creating a completely new experience, providing a way of communicating together and collaborate. Snapchat allowed people to communicate through ephemeral photos, TikTok through short videos, and Clubhouse through audio. So what kind of new experience can the future Web3 platforms allow?

3.1 - Solving the lock-in data problem

Decentralized social networks are unlike traditional social networks in that they're interface-agnostic. Indeed, one of the main advantages of Decentralized Social networks is the Interoperability they allow. In Web3, every transaction is taken on-chain (meaning send through a blockchain and verified by other people) and therefore accessible in an open ledger (all transactions happening in a blockchain are visible by anyone else). With its open data model, Crypto allows any Web3 platform to use those accessible data and, therefore, recover the user's Reputation from other platforms. A creator with 1M followers on a decentralized platform will bring them on any other Web3 platform. They are tied to their Crypto Wallet (Online identity) and not to a specific platform profile. Creators that have built an audience of 1 million followers on a Web3 platform won't start in another platform with 0 followers. They will begin with 1 million. Amazon sellers who have built their Reputation for years won't start on other marketplaces with 0 reviews. They will bring their Reputation across platforms and retrieve all their 5-stars reviews. It's a complete paradigm shift, and I admit it can be a difficult concept to understand. But similarly that you can access your email inbox from any computer in the world because it's tied to login and a password, not the computer itself, you'll be able to access your followers from any platform in the world because it's linked to your Crypto Wallet, not the platform itself.

Creators won't have their community's attention funneled through one platform but will be split up between interfaces. The sum of engagement across all interfaces will be greater than if it was a centralized platform.

To create a successful Decentralized Social Network, it's fundamental to allow Interoperability.

3.2 - Tokenized communities

The "holy grail" for Social Networks is creating a platform with Social Capital and Utility Simultaneously.

As shown in the graphic below, the more users coming on the platform, the more useful the platform becomes with the traditional network effect. No one would go on Instagram if there weren't the photos of their friends published there, on Uber if there wasn't any driver. With this model, any new platform needs to attract many users before the platform has any real utility...

On the other side, there's a new variable with the Token Network effect: The Financial utility. Indeed, even though there isn't much "application utility" initially, first users are incentivized through Social Tokens to use the platform and make it grow . A very high financial utility will drive new users to reach the inflection point where application utility will surpass the economic utility.

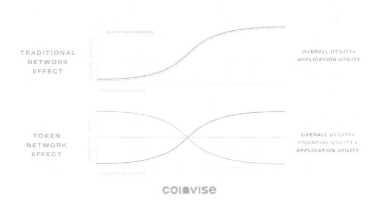

In decentralized social networks, users participate in the economic upside of the Network. They are rewarded for the time invested in building the product and Network. With the platform's utility increasing over time, more people will want to participate in its digital economy. The social token will gain value, rewarding early contributors for their hard work.

Decentralization is about profit-sharing and revenue tokenization. It combines utility (earning money) and social status. Users will come back and participate because it's actually good for them to participate in open economies. They will reach financial freedom and will gain social status within their tribe.

Decentralized Social Networks, in creating a token, will also play on the Proof-of-X mechanism. Users will do missions to earn the bounties (a single-player tool with multiplayer social feed), and the more the users use the app, the more likely they are to do the atomic behavior (more involved → more responsibilities → more missions → financial freedom).

Tokens will allow anyone to prove they are part of a community, prove that they've helped grow the community, and prove they were there since the beginning.

3.3 - Ads-driven problem

To succeed, a decentralized social network also needs to get rid of the old ads-driven business model.

In the end, brands are enterprise versions of creators. Today, one hundred advertisers drive 80% of Facebook's revenue. These are mega fortune 500 companies like P&G or Coca-Cola. They are doing that because it's (almost) the only solution to reach an audience, but they do not like what they have to do. They don't enjoy the game Facebook is playing with their billions of dollars and squeezing them for every penny.

These major brands feel the same pain as individual creators, and the next Decentralized social platforms need to solve this problem.

A great ads campaign is when you meet people where they are and understand what they need. Young people are not on Facebook anymore. If brands want to reach them, they have to be on Web3 and understand the trends. That's why Budweiser purchased the domain name "Beer.eth", VISA bought an NFT, and Arizona Ice Tea bought a Bored Ape. It's because they want to be part of this movement and reach the "cool kids."

Big brands like Arizona ice tea already understood that. They can't just show up to the party. They have to be invited and think very carefully about who they align with and how they grow together. There has to be a strong values alignment. It's more than ever crucial for brands to develop their brand and product so that Web3 communities will invite them in. Otherwise, those brands are going to be outsiders.

In building the next decentralized social Network, it's essential to understand these dynamics and align users' and brands' incentives. It seems like there is finally a viable business model that can suit both users and brands.

3.4 - Centralization problem

Maybe the next decentralized Social Network won't constitute one giant graph (similar to Facebook or Twitter) but constitutes many subgraphs around shared topics.

We're already seeing many communities and platforms collaborating, creating a Social network of many subgraphs. This seems to be a positive direction. It would be much harder to own, regulate, and moderate one giant decentralized Social Network.

The decentralization must also come within these sub-graphs. With the tokenization of these communities, the voting power (that comes with holding the token) will be split among many contributors and therefore limit the risks of a small group deciding for a whole community.

4 - Concrete use-cases

As mentioned at the beginning of this chapter, decentralized Social networks will succeed only if they allow to do things that can only be done on the Blockchain. It has to completely reinvent the user experience. It doesn't make sense to build a feed of photos and text "on the blockchain." It already exists on centralized social networks. In my opinion, even allowing users to "control their data" is not a strong enough selling point because users don't really see the advantages of their day-to-day use. For Web3 Social Network to succeed, the experience needs to be magic that is only possible on the Blockchain.

So what kind of experience is only possible on the Blockchain?

4.1 - The future of Media.

I think Media should leverage Web3 capabilities. A Magazine could create its own social Network. Indeed, it would imply a lot of advantages for the magazine and the users.

- **Check the sources** - With all the content now on-chain, it would be easy for anyone, even in ten years from now, to check the sources and double-check the information mentioned in an article.
- **Impossible to censor** - It will be impossible to censor someone as it's impossible to remove something from the Blockchain.
- **Raise funds easily** - The magazine could embed directly in their platform NFTs to raise money. Instead of going on another platform and creating an account, it will be easy for users to just click on the "Buy the NFT to support our work" button.
- **Track biggest fans** - It will also be easy for the magazine to track who helped the project and offer them special perks. We could imagine people buying the NFT receiving the ability to have access to exclusive content. As everything is on-chain, the NFT holders won't have to do anything. By signing up with their crypto wallet and, therefore, proving their identity, the platform will see they are the owner of the NFT and will unlock the content just for them. Even if they send the private link to their friends that don't hold the NFT, those friends won't be able to access it as the platform won't unlock the content.
- **Involve the community** - The magazine could also involve more of their community with democratic decisions by letting them vote through SnapShot.

4.2 - Building trust and empowering the next billions of curators.

Another interesting use case with decentralized Social networks is the ability to build a Social graph.

Again, as everything is on-chain and tied to someone's identity, it's easy for any web3 platform to access the data and create a Social Graph. That's something we've been working hard on at Coinvise. On every Coinvise creator profile, you can see the Social Tokens a creator owns and see which community they believe and participate in. Coinvise's creators also have a reputation score tied to their online identity and created based on their actions in other decentralized platforms.

Now imagine when there will be hundreds of creators and communities jumping into Web3. Any Coinvise user will have access to an on-chain social graph of the relationship between creators, their community, their work, their friends, etc...

It's a whole new world of possibilities for anyone wanting to discover new niches. Everyone will be a curator. Suppose you like a sport creator, for example. In that case, you'll be able to see directly in which community they believe in, in which ones they are participating in. All the information will be curated automatically. No need to do it manually. With an open-data model and every transaction happening on-chain, the curating work will be done automatically.

A decentralized Social Network could also solve the problem of trust. Today when selling on Facebook Marketplace or receiving DMs from people on Instagram, the only way to know if the person is legit is to trust weak social signals such as the number of followers, the profile picture, if the account is certified etc.. In web3, there will be the reputation score. Reputation_score will serve to establish trust for creators, not because they're high-signal on Twitter but because they've probably built and grow a high-value community. We'll explore this concept further in the next chapter of this book.

*

We're already seeing successful decentralized social Networks leveraging psychological mechanisms saw in this chapter and solving some of the most pressing problems with Web2 platforms. I can think of Showtime that allows its users to own their content through NFT (solve the lock-in data problem) and leveraging the Proof-of-X mechanism (by collecting rare NFTs, Showtime's users can prove their good taste (Proof-of-good-taste)). The platform also leveraged the "Investment-as-a-Status mechanism." It allows people to show that they have invested in a creator early, that they have been there since the beginning.

Rabbithole is also an interesting Web3 Platform that has implemented a "Proof-of-education" mechanism, letting its users prove they invested their time early in crypto. That leveraged the "Token Network effect" by rewarding its users with tokens when completing a quest.

I've also recently discovered two promising decentralized Social networks:

- XMPT - Breaking communication out of walled gardens and enabling messaging between wallets
- DeSo - DeSo is a new layer-1 blockchain built from the ground up to scale decentralized social applications to one billion users.

Web2 Social Networks will slowly lose all their users because they won't intrinsically solve the most pressing problems they are currently facing.

I think the next big social Network may start out not looking like a social network at all. There won't be one main social Network. There will be several social networks, all composable (more about composability in the next chapter).

We'll use daily several Web3 platforms and will bring our data to every one of them. There won't be a centralized power anymore, nor Lock-in data or ads-driven business model.

Crypto will be the native token for unlocking experience in these platforms and might be the native token for the Great Online Game, a sort of infinite video game that plays out constantly across the internet, where you're no longer playing as an avatar but playing as yourself across Twitter, YouTube. A game that rewards community and cooperation over individualism and competition.

And what if the next decentralized social network was simply the Metaverse?

16

Chapter 16: Reputation Score in Web3

Not so long ago, no one really cared about digital legitimacy and online reputation. There was way less collaboration happening online, and physical reputation was often sufficient to work efficiently with others. Managing a Digital identity and the reputation that goes with it was a nice-to-have, not a must-have, and was mostly limited to an email address and eventually a pseudo on several forums.

But as Vitalik Buterin, founder of Ethereum, said, "The Most Important Scarce Resource is Legitimacy." Legitimacy appears in any context where there is coordination, and especially on the Internet, coordination is everywhere. Nowadays, most of our day-to-day interactions and need for coordination exist in digital accounts, and our online reputation and legitimacy are more important than ever. Our real-life and digital life are intrinsically linked. People are now landing new jobs on Twitter, getting new clients on Linkedin, and collaborating with their co-workers on Slack.

Our digital identity is much more complex to manage than previously, and is formed at the intersection of different platforms, communities, and groups. So how to efficiently manage this online identity and build legitimacy?

We're already seeing solutions appearing on Web3. Web3 is defined as a decentralized web, where platforms have decentralized governance and open data compared to Web2, where platforms are mostly governed by centralized teams (CEO and key stakeholders) with lock-in data (you can't access the data of anyone on Facebook for example).

While it was complex to manage online identity and Reputation on Web2 because of Lock-in data and centralized power, Web3 and crypto mechanisms allow every action happening on the Blockchain (on-chain) to be linked to your unique decentralized identity, which means your reputation will follow you throughout your life. Put simply, thanks to crypto mechanisms, instead of having separate accounts on different platforms, you can now have a single account (online identity) that you can bring on different platforms. We're about to enter a new era where collaboration will be easier, and value creation will be rewarded thanks to an efficient reputation score.

1 - The problems with the current online Reputation

As mentioned above, our physical and digital lives are intrinsically linked, and online reputation is more important than ever. However, for 99% of people on the Internet, the value of their digital identity is locked within platforms. Creators that have built an audience of 1 million followers on Instagram won't start in another platform like Twitter with 1 million followers. They will begin with 0. Amazon sellers who have built their Reputation for years won't start on other marketplaces with five-star reviews. They will begin with 0. When leaving a platform, users have to start from scratch, all over again, as there is no interoperability between platforms. The data are locked. It doesn't incentivize users to do their best or build long-term relationships as they know they will lose it when leaving the platform.

The second problem with the current online reputations is the negligible cost of creating a new online identity. To create a whole model around reputation, we've to be sure who's the person behind this pseudonymous or this email address. Today, anyone can create new accounts for no cost, limiting the weight we can put behind a name or a pseudo.

Interoperability, open data, and a reliable way to know someone's identity are essential to create a legit reputation score, and Web2 platforms have failed to provide those key elements.

2 - Interoperability and reputation score on Web3

Thanks to crypto mechanisms and Crypto Wallets, we can now all have a unique decentralized identity that can be used across different platforms. We finally see the path to create a reputation score.

Every transaction (and by transaction, we don't specifically talk about monetary transactions, it can be social ones as well) happening on the Blockchain are registered on a public ledger and are accessible to anyone. To do transaction on the Blockchain, everyone needs a Crypto Wallet to be identified. Similarly than you need a credit card to purchase an item online, you need a Crypto Wallet to do transactions on the Blockchain, with the difference that you can also use your Wallet to do non-financial transactions. It's like if you could use your credit card to sign up on new websites.

THE SOCIAL TOKEN REVOLUTION

Web3 platforms allow using a wallet as a single sign-on. Like the "connect with Google" button, you now have a "connect with your Wallet" button. By gaining access to every new user's identity through their Crypto Wallet, Web3 platforms will be able to track a specific user's action and reward them for creating value.

With crypto Wallets, the problem of fake online identity is solved. You can create a new address email at a negligible cost, but with your identity linked to your Wallet (already connected to a lot of Dapp (Decentralized applications) and with your virtual currencies and your NFTs in it), it will be much more difficult for someone to create several identities. The cost of creating a new wallet will be too high and the benefits too low.

Now comes the need of Interoperability. In Web3 As every transaction is taken on-chain and therefore accessible in an open ledger, Crypto wallet finally also allows interoperability. With its open data model (every information is on a public ledger), Crypto allows any Web3 platforms to use those data and, therefore, recover the user's reputation from other platforms. For example, if a user sent many messages on Discord, it's a good sign that the user is engaged in a community. If a user has participated in several community's crowdfunding, it shows its support in different communities. Publishing essays on decentralized platforms shows the willingness to provide value and help others etc... All those "transactions" are visible on the public ledger, everything is "on-chain." You can go on another platform or software, and the platform can recover all your information and past transactions. In the new world of Ethereum and Web3, your identity and data go with you.

We've just seen that Crypto solves the two main problems of centralized platforms, and that it's now possible to create a reputation score thanks to open data, interoperability, and a single decentralized identity.

So now, concretely, what would be the advantages of having a web3 reputation score?

3 - Main advantages of a Web3 Reputation score

There are many advantages to having a Web3 reputation score. Firstly, it acts as a metric for On-chain participation, creation & ownership. It helps identify high-value creators/communities & access a better quality talent pool for communities to onboard. In many ways, a reputation score will serve to establish trust for creators, not because they're high-signal on Twitter but because they've probably built a high-value community. With interoperability and reputation Score, Web3 platforms and communities will be able to reward those who create the most value. Reputation scores incentivize creation and participation.

A reputation score on Web3 has many advantages that we'll list here:

- **Self-sovereignty** - users own their online identity and reputation. Web3 platforms do not lock their data, and they are the only ones with access to their Wallet and all proof of their identity and past actions.
- **Portability & interoperability** - Users are allowed to move their data into other systems and platforms. On Web3, anyone could bring its audience or content from a platform to another.
- **Allow to find high-quality people** - Users and communities will work with people who have a high reputation score. A reputation score will incentivize everyone to create more value and help each other.
- **Better governance distribution** - Today, we mostly use users' number of tokens to give voting power. In the future, it could be directly your reputation score that serves to determine your voting

power. It won't be enough to buy a lot of tokens. You'll have to prove your value to gain voting power.

- **Establish trust** - With a life-long reputation, users will be more likely to play the infinite game, where the objective is not to win but to keep playing. As everything is on-chain, users will be incentivized to do good, ultimately resulting in more trust.
- **Incentivize to create more value** - Users will be incentivized to help each other without fearing losing their reputation when joining new communities or projects. Someone with a high reputation score will be able to join new projects and prove its past experiences and capabilities right away.

*

The reputation score is the first attempt to establish trust for creators, showcase them, and reward those who create the most value. By having a verified identity on platforms that have implemented such a system as Coinvise (Wallet + Twitter), creators will be confident that the value they are creating with their community and their reputation will follow them across platforms.

It's time to leverage new technologies to give users control of their digital identity and allow them to bring their reputation across platforms.

17

Chapter 17: Monetization in Web3

Monetization has always been a top priority for Creators.

After they discovered from 00' to 10's they could monetize their audience through Web2 platforms and that it was possible to earn a living from their passion, Creators then realized from 10' to 20 they could actually BE the brand, BE the product, and could do for them what they were doing for others.

Indeed, the emergence of new technologies cumulated to a paradigm shift in how GenZs see the work has led us to a new era for creators.

Crypto, and tokens specifically, seem to be the path to help these creators achieve financial freedom and live from their passion, creating content online. Even major Creator-focused Web2 companies already understood. Tokens can revolutionize how creators make money online. Patreon is already looking into crypto tokens as another way for creators to monetize communities.

So how and why tokens, through Ownership and direct value creation, will replace the old ads/brand sponsorship monetization framework? And how will creators leverage this technology and monetize their audience compared to the traditional way? That's what we're going to find out in this chapter.

1 - The current Monetization model in Web2.

As we already explored in the first part of this book, the Creator Economy results from a complete paradigm shift in the way more people, and GenZs specifically, are seeing the work. It's indeed more and more common to post on the internet, share photos, join forums, curate articles and make money out of it. The internet levels the playing field, and anyone can use their hustle and savvy to amass a following and monetize that following.

However, there are still two major problems for creators today: Ownership and Monetization.

Creators don't have Ownership because of the ads-driven business model most Web2 social platforms, where creators build their audience, are using. Indeed, in Web2, the process of monetization for platform usually goes something like this:

1. Company launches an app
2. It onboards as many users as possible
3. Then it monetizes its user base

But this outdated business model forces current social networks to keep a walled garden around their content. Indeed, opening their data would mean killing their business model. Their main way to monetize is to sell those data to for-profit companies to target specific audiences. This business model gives users and creators no choice but to continue using these apps as they have already created an audience on these platforms.

On top of that, this business model creates a situation where creators who actually produce the content are underpaid, under-monetized, and don't fully capture the value they are making.

With this broken ads-driven Business Model, creators don't have much choice but to rent the audience they don't really own to brands keen to pay a lot of money to access it. As you can imagine, this model is unsustainable for creators, and we need to give them back Ownership over their content and ways to monetize it more efficiently.

2 - The first era of monetization in Web3.

There's a famous essay written by Kevin Kelly called "1,000 True Fans," predicting that the internet would allow more people to make a living off their creations. Rather than pursuing widespread celebrity, he argued, creators only needed to engage a modest base of "true fans"—those who will "buy anything you produce"—to the tune of $100 per fan per year (for a total annual income of $100,000). Li Jin later argued creators would eventually need only 100 true fans to make a living off their passion.

I believe Li Jin is right. New crypto technologies allow creators to monetize their content more efficiently. In recent months, and with creators becoming increasingly aware of Web3's capabilities, we saw more of them experimenting with new monetization models and earning life-changing money.

While there are many ways for creators to leverage the crypto technology

, it seems there are two main ways for them to monetize more efficiently their content:

- **Creating a Token that gives access to premium content** - Fans (or community members) can buy a token and get access to content in advance, access token-gated content such as private channels in a Discord or the "Close Friends" on Instagram. The Token allows to limit access at scale and provide recognition and status for the biggest fans within the community.
- **Allowing fans to invest in the Creator through a Token** - With the Creator becoming more famous, more people want to buy the Token to get access to exclusive content, and the token increases in value. Fans can redeem coins, treating them as an investment, and creators can eventually use the liquidity to buy new materials, create better quality content and augment its distribution. In this case, the Token serves as a way to crowdfund the creator.

Mainstream creators are today mostly using Non-fungible Tokens (aka NFTs) to monetize their content as they are allowing many new use-cases (explained just above). NFTs also come with status, scarcity, and belonging within the community.

With these new tokens (NFTs) that creators can now create easily, comes the concept of Ownership for fans and creators. As Jesse Walden says in his essay *The Ownership Economy:Crypto & The Next Frontier of Consumer Software*: "Rather than a platform's inner circle of founders and investors taking home the value, users can earn the majority of value generated from their collective contributions." It allows creators to monetize their content while involving their community and aligning incentives. Fans can purchase tokens which allow creators to don't rely exclusively on the revenue generated by Web2 platforms (Youtube ads for example), and creators, through the token, give ownership to fans by sharing with them the upsides of their content. That's the magic of Ownership.

When creators give real Ownership to their community, community members start to take care of it, and engagement often follows. Aligning incentives is everything.

By creating a token and leveraging Web3 tools, creators can more easily foster a sustainable community (less spam), ensures members have skin in the game (not only passive members or commenters), and incentivizes community members to make the overall community desirable to join over the long-term (the more desirable the community, the more value the Token will gain).

Putting these new technologies in the hands of creators is a great step forward over Ownership. Indeed, while in Web2, creators needed engagement to attract ad revenue, in Web3, monetization and engagement happen at the same time. Users engage in Web3 with their capital by buying an NFT for example. Since day one, it allows creators to get revenue, allowing them to monetize their content more easily even without a large audience and to bring their audience out of Web2 platforms.

By purchasing the Creator's Token, fans further commit to their favorite creators and build a positive feedback loop that nurtures healthy fan communities built around a shared passion. In the end, tokens provide a way for super fans to show their loyalty and provide initial liquidity for creators.

While mainstream creators minting NFTs for their community is insanely exciting, I feel like creators can go even further and completely reinvent how they see monetization. Instead of adapting old models to fit the Web3 space, creators could try completely new monetization models that Web3 allows.

By leveraging fungible tokens (aka Social tokens or Community tokens) and reinventing what it means to be a Creator, I think there is a possible future where anyone could live from their passion, owning 100% of their content and making what they love.

3 - The second era of monetization in Web3.

While, until now, the term "Creator" (or before that "influencers") was mostly tied to people creating content online, it seems like Web3 allows a whole new class of Creators to emerge. These new creators are people who share their vision through content online rather than creating content as an end goal. A Web3 creator's definition could be:

"Anyone pushing ideas, and a vision, through content on the internet and leveraging the new Web3 tools at their disposal."

This broader definition includes more people under the term "creator" and reflects more on these individuals' actions. These "Creators 2.0" might be the one that benefits the most from the Web3 revolution. Again, as we've already explored previously in this book, Jeff Kauffman Jr is a perfect example of a Creator 2.0. Jeff, which might not be considered a creator in a traditional sense, has created a thriving community around advertising and marketing in Web3. He's pushing his ideas and vision through essays and podcasts, gathering a strong community keen to help him achieve his high ambition goals. Creating content is not its end goal. Its end goal is to share its vision and gather a community around it.

These Creators 2.0 are not trying to move their already existing audience into Web3 to monetize it better. They are creating new communities using Web3 tools and leveraging their previous following. And there's a huge difference between an audience and a community.

In 2021, we've already seen many thriving communities led by Creators 2.0. For example, I can think of Carlos Gomes that has created Forefront, a community that recently raised $2.1M to Build the "Port of Entry" to Web3 Social Clubs & Digital Cities. Another great example is Friends With Benefits, led by the Creator Trevor McFedries, which recently finalized its $10M fundraise at a $100M valuation led by Andreessen Horowitz.

These creators are not monetizing their audience in a Web2 way. They are building tokenized communities to create projects that bring real value and then monetize this project.

Today, to build a startup, someone needs money in order to hire people and support themselves. They usually raise this money from VC firms and give away a percentage of the company. This investment introduces misaligned incentives, and even if the company succeeds, it will take a long time for anyone involved to realize any real return on investment.

A contrario, with Social tokens, these Creators 2.0 can build solid projects and incentivize their audience to participate in investing money or time in it from day one, avoiding raising money from investors. With Social Tokens as equities, fans will put in some work and get rewarded with Tokens, letting them redeem perks in the project's virtual economy or by selling them for USD later if the project succeeds.

Even if the project needs to raise proper money, it can do it through the community. Stakeholders can then use their tokens to vote on future strategic decisions, and the people who helped build the project can sell some of their holdings to make money after the tokens have been released. People who believe in the project can buy and hold Ownership, and people who think the project is headed in the wrong direction can signal this by selling their stakes. Anyway, purchasers have complete transparency over what is happening as everything is on-chain.

In Web3, community members own a part of the Creator's content and success through tokens. As they benefit directly from the growth of the Creator, they are incentivized to provide help.

Social Tokens, in the end, allow to align interests, get workforce from day one, facilitate collaboration with community members, and monetize more efficiently.

4 - The problems we still have to overcome.

But no solution is perfect, and there are still a lot of improvements that can be made to improve monetization in Web3 through Tokens.

When monetizing through tokens, creators have to make their content appealing to fans, not brands. They have to produce much better quality content to delight the fans, as they are the ones spending the money. Monetizing via attention, which is what creators in Web2 are doing, means producing a lot of lower-quality content, prioritizing quantity over quality (more videos > more ads> more revenues). On the other end, monetizing from superfans is a much higher barrier to entry to starting earning as creators always have to be innovative and create better quality content. Marketing for money, not attention, completely changes how creators are producing content.

The second problem is the Discoverability Dilemma. Do creators want to be discovered by a larger audience and let their content for free, or do they prefer to token-gate their content, driving revenue but losing invisibility? Web2 platforms, which have a large user-base and control discoverability, will always be the place for casual creators (the mass majority) who are simply looking to monetize the attention they generate. To make the tokens a long-term viable way to monetize content, we have to introduce a new way to drive attention for creators without relying on centralized platforms. Building decentralized Social Networks might be a solution to explore. Incentivizing the biggest fans to share the content by rewarding them with Token could be another way to tackle the discoverability dilemma, while it doesn't have the scale of millions of users' platforms for now.

Lastly, how do Creators get liquidity from their Tokens? Currently, there is nothing in place for them to "take salary" without selling their coin, which seems not aligned with long-term community interests. Likewise for contributors, which have to trash the coin to get their salary when contributing to the community, lose voting power in the process. To improve monetization through tokens, we need to implement new tools or mechanisms to help the creators and community members' get paid' without selling their coins. One potential solution could be to create two tokens, one for paying salaries and rewarding community members, the other for governance power and perks within the community.

*

Through this chapter, we saw that Web3 could help Creators 1.0 and Creators 2.0 monetize their content more efficiently. While there is no perfect solution yet, more and more creators are leveraging crypto mechanisms and are building thriving communities. To allow the next million creators to live from their passion, we'll have to think together about creating efficient monetization models. Building Web3 tools seem to be the more promising path for now.

18

Conclusion

Throughout this book, we've explored many fundamentals concepts.

We've firstly explained the Web3 basics, understanding the keywords of Web3, what DAOs are, and how they can reinvent the way we work. We then described how to leverage the social Token technology through a series of "How to guide," exploring the different steps anyone would have to get involved in thriving DAOs. In the third part of this book, we deep-dived into the technical aspects of a Social Token, explaining how to use financial tools easily. We finally explored how Social Tokens play into our lives in the next couple of years and new use-cases that will emerge.

The use-cases and advantages are numerous, and education will play a significant role in the future years. It's up to us to develop this technology and make it mainstream. If you've made it until here, you should now be part of the 99.9% of people that understand how Social Tokens work.

We're still, however, highly early in the Social Tokens revolution, and some concepts we talked about in this book might be outdated or have disappeared in a couple of years. There are, for example, several reasons interoperability will not happen overnight and may never happen at scale (privacy, security, and moderation...). Some limits remain to unleash the mass adoption of Social tokens. We can think of high transaction fees, the difficulty of managing a crypto wallet, and the scarcity of talent in the space for example.

These aspects are improving fast, and I'm convinced Social Tokens will become more and more users soon. We're already seeing 500 Fortune companies buying NFTs and famous artists leveraging this technology to unlock new experiences with their fans.

We're living in exciting times, and you're now part of this movement.

We're all going to make it.

Use-case #1: $ELIOT - A community-driven education token

Since I'm working at Coinvise, my goal has always been to educate and onboard new people into Web3 and Crypto. Innovation in Crypto (DAOs, NFT, Defi, Web3 & Social Tokens) has led us to a new era that will revolutionize almost every area of our lives, from how we make money to how we collaborate.

Education plays a significant role in the mass adoption of all those new concepts, and I want to help make this one-in-a-generation change happen.

As more people are leaping Web3, I receive many questions and requests on how to break into this space. My goal is to leverage the power of the community to onboard these new people, as I can't answer all the questions myself anymore.

It's a positive sum-game where we all have an interest in onboarding new people in the space and where helping someone today might lead to new opportunities tomorrow.

While this Token is very new and we'll create more interesting experimentation together in the future, I've created the Token for three main reasons:

1- Helping anyone to become hooked in the Social Token space

2- Understand the use cases by actually experimenting

3- Incentivize community members to help me grow within the space.

In this chapter, I'll explore the vision for the $ELIOT Token - a community-driven education token to incentivize education and collaboration in Web3 platforms. Let's dig more into this.

1- Helping anyone to become hooked in the Social Token space

After I took the leap into Web3 and understood better the capabilities of such a technology, it seems inevitable that Web3 will become mainstream. Some 500 Fortune have entered this space, such as Budweiser, who purchased the domain name "Beer.eth", VISA, which bought an NFT, and Arizona Ice Tea, which purchased a Bored Ape.

With this first experiment, my goal is to onboard people to understand the use cases of Social Tokens. I've written many essays, played podcasts, and participated in conferences to discuss Social Tokens' use-cases. Still, I'm convinced there is no better way to learn than actually doing things. Some concepts such as interoperability or Reputation Score can be tricky to understand theoretically, and newcomers in the space can feel overwhelmed by all the information.

This is the reason why I've created the $ELIOT and the "$ELIOT HQ" space on Coinvise's Discord. With this space dedicated to learning and onboarding new individuals to Web3, we'll together leverage the "Learn-to-Earn" model as well as the power of a community and the Token Network Effect.

1.1 Learn-to-Earn model

This space will leverage the "Learn-to-Earn" model, where people will be able to earn $ELIOT by proving they have accomplished the missions. With this, I hope to incentivize more individuals to actually DO things to learn. You can already complete several missions, and a strong community of nearly 1000 members is ready to help you and answer your question in Coinvise's Discord.

1.2 Leverage the community

At Coinvise, we're a community-first platform. In my opinion, community-driven courses (and cohort-based courses) are the best to learn new things effectively. I've experienced this way of learning while being at OnDeck and saw how people were supporting each other, helping each other, and sharing exciting resources. That's the reason why I want to create a safe place where everyone helps each other.

The "ELIOT HQ" is not a DAO where you have to commit many hours/week or a place where there are high-level projects. See it more as a fun experiment, a group of friends interested in the same things and keen to help each other.

Once the first members are onboarded and have achieved the first missions, I hope that they will help others and create a positive feedback loop.

1.3 - The Token Network Effect

The goal is also to validate the hypothesis that we can build together an educational place (ELIOT HQ) while adding a social component on top of it and leveraging the Token network effect, where people first come to earn tokens and then stay for the community.

Again, with the Token Network effect, even though there isn't much "application utility" initially, first users are incentivized through Social Tokens to come in the community (ELIOT HQ) and make it grow.

2 - How does it work?

Each individual dropping its Ethereum address in the Discord Server will receive 50 $ELIOT. This first mission is a way to incentivize more people to create a Crypto Wallet and make the leap into Crypto. These 50 tokens will serve as currency in the digital ELIOT economy. Every user will be able to do quests, discover, and interact with different Web3 platforms (Mirror, Snapshot, Collab.Land etc..).

To join the experience, anyone can:

- Join the Coinvise's Discord Server.
- Head over the "$ELIOT HQ" space and read the "Start-here" channel.
- Start doing quests and interact in the different channels (share articles, help others, ask questions etc..)

There will be a weekly airdrop to reward the users who have shared their Ethereum addresses, helpful to the community, and completed missions. More details about the number of tokens allocated to each quest are available directly on the Discord Server.

Some of the quests you'll be able to accomplish by joining the $ELIOT HQ:

- **Import a Token:** Learn how to import a Token on Metamask by adding Polygon to your Wallet and importing $ELIOT.
- **Coinvise quest:** Discover Coinvise, claim rewards, learn how to follow other creators, and create a token.
- **Create a Wallet:** Learn how to create a Wallet and share your address with others.
- **Purchase this book and leave a review**

This initial experimentation will run for a month and will then be paused to let me reflect on the experience. Again, this is the first experiment that runs with the $ELIOT token, and I'm sure the purpose of this Token will evolve in the following months.

The goal with $ELIOT is to create a digital currency in a whole virtual economy where anyone will be free to experiment with the joy of Web3 without spending real money.

3- What will you be able to do with your $ELIOT, and how to earn them?

To earn $ELIOT, you'll have to accomplish some of the missions I've created in the ELIOT HQ (starting with the ones listed above). I'll also send $ELIOT to whoever interacts in the different channels and is helpful to the community.

At some point, I want to reward the early supporters of this experimentation and will therefore offer perks to $ELIOT holders (still need to figure out the minimum amount of Token required for these). I'll allow early supporters to:

- Access my latest essays before anyone else.
- Get a 30min call with me to ask me anything Social-Token-related.
- Receive sneak-pic of a big project I'm working on.
- Get a coffee with me in San Francisco.
- More perks to come...

At this point, you should have enough information to start your Web3 journey. Can't wait to see you in the Discord and see what comes out from this experimentation.

Use case #2: Why SuperTeam DAO should create a Token.

In this chapter, I will explore what Superteam DAO is building to better understand their potential needs. I will then explain the benefits of creating Social Tokens for a DAO and continue this chapter by outlining how Superteam DAO could grow even more and achieve their highly ambitious goal thanks to Social Tokens.

1 - What is SuperTeam DAO?

Super Team DAO is a co-operative of operators helping the most promising Solana projects launch and grow in the ascending world.
Three key characteristics define them:

- **They are serving as an aggregator** - Superteam DAO connects the dots between teams building on Solana, high-quality talents looking to help, and investors looking to invest and develop the ecosystem.
- **They are building the talent layer for Solana** - The DAO wants to accelerate adoption for the next billion crypto users by creating a talent pool that Solana projects can tap to launch and grow their dApps.
- **They are targeting the ascending world (India, South East Asia,**

Eastern Europe, and Africa) - Their goal is to find high-quality talents in those countries, teach them how to code, and recruit them later to help build, launch and grow projects on Solana.

What's really exciting about Superteam DAO is that they decided to create a DAO to pursue their vision instead of creating a traditional company.

They are organized not as a pyramidal structure where the top half of the organization monetizes the bottom half. Instead, they choose to be more like a creative operative, where every member is free to work on what they like, contribute as much as they want to, and receive corresponding ownership in the networks and projects they help. It's a complete paradigm shift in the way people collaborate.

Instead of building a traditional company, they have gathered a strong community of talented people and have created a Service DAO around this community. Service DAO is a proven business model with a radically new operating model, where no intermediary is taking a cut on every transaction. Instead, we could see a Service DAO as a friendly virtual place where everyone can connect with and help each other. The goal of a service DAO is to create a strong network effect to become the go-to place to meet people in the Solana ecosystem.

By gathering a strong community of talents and operators passionate about the Solana ecosystem, Superteam DAO is creating a virtual economy with a positive feedback loop.

We now have a better understanding of Superteam DAO' vision and needs, and we could summarize these in an easy list.

- Superteam DAO needs to improve coordination between collabora-tors across many countries (ascending world).
- They need to manage a whole ecosystem with several stakeholders, connect the dots and be flexible.
- At some point, they will have to distribute ownership in the network and incentivize more people to collaborate.
- On a daily basis, they need a way to reward core contributors for their work and give them voting power.
- Lastly, they need to incentivize more people to join the Solana ecosystem so they can tap into a larger pool of talent and interesting projects.

2 - Why Superteam DAO should create a Token.

One of the major problems Superteam DAO will face if they want to achieve their high ambitious goal to become the go-to place to work in the Solana ecosystem is the coordination between contributors across countries. Indeed, Superteam DAO targets the ascending world (India, South East Asia, Eastern Europe, and Africa), and all those potential contributors have very little in common. They are not in the same timezone, have never met each other, don't use the same currency in their daily lives, and the chance they will trust each other to collaborate on projects is close to zero.

On top of the struggle to coordinate contributors across countries, Superteam DAO also coordinates several other stakeholders. Indeed, to create a whole ecosystem and a founder network around Solana, they need to make sure the communication between teams, talents, and investors is fluid and easy.

Since its inception, the team has understood the importance of building a strong community first, and they've been greatly successful in growing this community day after day. But soon, they will have to think thoroughly about organizing, coordinating, and rewarding this growing community.

The easiest way to solve this problem seems to create a Social Token. Let's dig more into how Social Tokens can help solve some of the needs of the Superteam DAO team.

2.1 - Improve coordination between collaborators across many countries (ascending world)

As explained in the second part of this chapter, Social tokens have the significant advantage of facilitating the coordination between contributors. Indeed, with Social Tokens, anyone can easily set up governance power, token-gate channels at scale, send tips easily, and pay contributors across the globe in one click.

With a Token, the key decisions could be taken on-chain. It would be easy to reward the contributors by doing one monthly airdrop even though they are worldwide. The Token would serve as a digital currency and allow for rewarding contributors working on smaller-scale projects, accomplishing small missions that help Superteam DAO grow.

2.2 - Leveraging the Token Network Effect

The main goal of the DAO is to create a co-operative of operators helping the most promising Solana projects launch & grow in the ascending world. They want to match investors, developers, and world-class talents to collaborate together and grow the ecosystem.

But to do, they might face the same problem that two-side marketplaces are facing. How do you convince projects to join your community if you don't have a pool of talents that can help them succeed, and how do you gather a strong community of talent if you don't have any projects to make them work on?

With a Social Token, the DAO could leverage the Token Network Effect.

As shown in the graphic below, with the traditional network effect, the more users coming on the platform, the more useful the platform becomes. With this old model, it's very complicated at the beginning for any new platform to attract enough new users and see the platform becoming useful.

On the other side, there's a new variable with the Token Network effect: The Financial utility. Indeed, even though there isn't much "application utility" initially, first users are incentivized through Social Tokens to use the platform and make it grow. A very high financial utility will drive new users to reach the inflection point where application utility will surpass the economic utility.

In these decentralized communities leveraging the Token Network effect, users participate in the economic upside of the DAO. They are rewarded for the time invested in building the community and growing the ecosystem. With the community's utility increasing over time, more people will want to participate in its digital economy. The social Token will gain value, rewarding early contributors for their hard work.

Decentralization is about profit-sharing and revenue tokenization. It combines utility (earning money) and social status. Users will come back and participate because it's actually good for them to participate in open economies. They will reach financial freedom and will gain social status within their tribe.

2.3 - Manage an ecosystem with several stakeholders and give contributors voting power.

Superteam DAO's workers completing missions are currently paid in the $NAME token of the project they've helped. This system completely makes sense, as it's a way to incentivize the contributors to do their best work (the tokens they receive will grow in value over time if the project succeeds) and a way to prove the team is serious and is keen to pay people for their help. Aligning incentives is everything.

However, to manage the whole ecosystem Superteam DAO is creating, the team would greatly benefit from creating a token. Indeed, a token would serve to incentivize contributors to work for Superteam DAO itself, finding new talents, new projects to collaborate with, new partnerships, etc... To achieve their goal, Superteam DAO will need different teams (ops, comm, design). Creating a Social Token for the DAO seems to be the only way to align incentives with the contributors and allow their early believers to share the upsides.

The ecosystem wouldn't use a top/down approach where only a few people decide for this project's future, but it would be community-led. Anyone would have ownership, which will, in the end, reward the most promising projects and not the ones that only a small group of people would have voted for.

Voting power would also serve to take critical decisions over the different experiments. Superteam DAO currently has a podcast, a YouTube channel, a Substack, etc...

A Social Token could:

- Serve as a way for contributors to vote on the future of those projects, maybe voting on potential future contents and initiatives to develop these media.
- Be a great way to incentivize more people to speak in the podcast and hook them into the ecosystem (by rewarding them with Tokens).
- Be a great way to incentivize the community to design thumbnails, reach out to potential guests, or recap the conversations.

*

After spending hours digging through what Superteam DAO is doing, I fully realized how ambitious their project is. To succeed, this project needed to be a DAO. It couldn't exist as a traditional company. It would have been too complicated to coordinate this ecosystem with traditional tools and hierarchy. Only the fact that anyone can jump in, submit new ideas, and start developing the space makes Superteam DAO super valuable. But to bring their vision even further, they need a token to fuel the ecosystem they are creating.

Throughout this chapter, we've shown why and how Superteam DAO would greatly benefit from creating a Token and how it would help the team overcome some of their most pressing problems while opening a world of new possibilities to develop the ecosystem and the community they are creating.

Crypto's Lexicon

Blockchain: A blockchain is a digital ledger that stores all the transactions in a decentralized and secure way thanks to cryptographic mechanisms. Instead of relying on third parties such as banks to serve as the middleman in a transaction, you can securely send money without having to trust the recipient by doing it on a Blockchain. Every action taken on the Blockchain must be verified by others to be approved, making sure there is no fraud.

Crypto Wallet: The same way you have banking information that you share with anyone that wants to send you money, a crypto wallet creates and stores your Private & Public Keys (a series of numbers similar to your banking information) that allows you to send and receive money on the Blockchain. You'll use your Public Key as Banking information, while your Private Key will serve to verify and validate the transactions. A Crypto Wallet is from where you'll be able to send/request cryptocurrencies and see how much crypto you have.

Decentralized Autonomous Organizations (DAO): DAOs have emerged in recent years, allowing people to collaborate on smaller-scale projects than companies. DAOs are organized around a mission that coordinates through a shared set of rules enforced on a blockchain. Put it simply, DAOs are a new way to finance projects, govern communities, and share value.

Gas fees: Gas Fee is a term used to describe the transaction fee taken by the Ethereum blockchain upon the execution of a smart contract. Every transaction happening on the Ethereum Blockchain needs to be verified by others to be approved. Users that verify the transactions are called "Miners" and to thank those contributors (Miners) for verifying a transaction and incentivizing them to make the network more secure, we give them a tip, a slice of the trade, also called "Gas fees." You can find the price of the Gas fees on EtherScan. The fractional denomination of Ether used when referring to gas prices is "Gwei." A reasonably "good price" can range between 20 to 30 Gwei. Gas fees are often exceeding these numbers.

Non-fungible token (NFT): Non-fungible token (NFT) is a term used to describe a unique digital asset whose ownership is tracked on a blockchain, such as Ethereum. Assets that can be represented as NFTs range from digital goods, such as items that exist within virtual worlds, to claims on physical assets such as clothing items or real estate.

Social Token: A social token is a digital currency that lives in a virtual economy. Anyone can create their own Social Token and incentivize people to work in exchange for this Token. Social Tokens, finally, make it easier to collaborate on smaller-scale projects and help create trust between parties. Instead of setting up contracts and legal status to cover each contributor, Social Tokens allow doing transactions on a blockchain, meaning enforced by crypto mechanisms, in a trustful way.

Web3: The terms "Web3" or "Decentralized Web" are slowly taking over "crypto." Web3 is a broader term that comes without the 2017 baggage of the word "Crypto." Indeed, "Crypto" is too often associated with "scam" and "speculation." Instead, the term "Web3" is more reminiscent of the evolution of the internet as we know it today, solving the most pressing problems of Web2 platforms through Crypto mechanisms.

About the Author

Eliot is a french writer passionate about Social Token, Web3 & Creator economy. He works as a Community & Content Creator at Coinvise where he helps Web3 Creators & Communities Build Open Economies.

You can connect with me on:

🌐 https://www.eliotcouvat.com

🐦 https://twitter.com/CDTEliot

Subscribe to my newsletter:

✉ https://eliotc.substack.com

Printed in Great Britain
by Amazon

76251264R00102